Whatever Happened to Hell?

by
JON E. BRAUN

Thomas Nelson Publishers
Nashville • New York

Library of Congress Cataloging in Publication Data

Braun, Jon E
  Whatever happened to hell?

  Bibliography: p. 191
  Includes index.
  1. Hell. I. Title.
BT836.2.B7   236'.25   79-218
ISBN 0-8407-5158-3

CONTENTS

I am the way into the city of woe.
I am the way to a forsaken people.
I am the way into eternal sorrow.

Sacred Justice moved my architect.
I was raised here by divine omnipotence,
Primordial love and ultimate intellect.

Only those elements time cannot wear
Were made before me, and beyond time I stand.
Abandon all hope ye who enter here.*

*The words Dante Alighieri (1265-1321) had inscribed over the
gates of hell in *The Inferno*.

Whatever Happened to Hell?

1
Making Light of Darkness_____

It is not unlikely that within the last twenty-four hours you've heard someone say, "What the hell are you doing?" Or, "I sure as hell will." Or, "Who in the hell do you think you are?"

That word *hell* has become a conversational byword in our day. Good friends dare to say playfully to one another, "Go to hell." They surely don't mean, "Go to the place of punishment for the wicked after death," though that is how the dictionary defines the word *hell*.

But why use the word *hell?* Why not instead, "What the jail are you doing?" Or, "I sure as school will." And why not say, "Oh, go to Chicago"? Simply because *jail, school,* and *Chicago,* even for the enemies of each, have no real sting. They have only the flavor of vanilla at a time when chocolate or peppermint is needed.

When it comes right down to it, in the English language, *hell* is the strongest expletive available that carries the idea of ultimate deprivation, devastation, fear, torment, punishment, suffering, and loss. Whether or not the user of the term *hell* believes in an actual, literal hell is of little or no consequence. There is an inbuilt, inarticulated, yet understood bite in the very word itself.

So if hell really is the place for eternal punishment of the wicked after death, how come it's used so lightly millions and millions of times each day? Why is there such an apparent lack of seriousness about the word? Why is a word so heavy with meaning used so indifferently? Why do people pretend the place doesn't exist?

When is the last time you heard a serious sermon on the subject or read an article of note dealing with judgment and eternal punishment? Even the evangelical crowd has, by and large, avoided the topic—opting for a more "positive" approach. Hell has come on hard times.

Deep below the surface of things, a proliferating erosion concerning the seriousness of hell, brought on by a complex web of modern ideas about hell, has stripped this weighty word of most of its awesomely solemn content.

Moderns and Hell

Frivolous modern notions about hell have arisen to compete with what the people of God have for centuries understood and believed about the unending punishment of the wicked. The threat of having multitudes of people deceived into taking hell lightly is greater now than it has ever been in human history.

Consider five samples of modern belief about hell that any one of us might be exposed to. A brief look at these prevalent, popular ideas helps show how the modern mind deals with hell.

Hell on Earth

How amazingly common it is these days to hear someone express the idea that hell is an experience limited to earth and this life. When asked recently what he thought about hell, a meat salesman in the South replied, "Hell is here on earth. The badder you are, the worse it is. There is good in all of us, and that goes to heaven. The bad stays here."[1]

Less committal was the mortgage broker who said he felt that hell was here on earth, then added, "I'm not sure that we don't make our own hell. At least we probably contribute to it."[2]

The "Hell-on-earthers" agree that there must be some form of negative consequence for wrongdoing because justice demands some retribution for evil. But they insist those consequences are

---

[1]*The Nashville Banner,* 22 May 1978, p. 33.
[2]Ibid.

specifically a "this-life" affair. The possibility of eternal punishment in an afterlife existence is either dismissed as highly unlikely, or ignored because "it just doesn't seem that it should be that way."

It Can't Be All That Bad

There is a large contingent of moderns who have the unsettling suspicion that there is a hell in the hereafter. But, no worry, "it couldn't be all that bad." Certainly, it isn't as good a place as heaven, but it isn't bad enough to make it worth giving up the sinful things in this life just to avoid going there.

Those with this view see the difference between heaven and hell as one only of degrees of something basically good.

It is hard to be convinced that this notion is much more than a wistful hope that "things won't be as bad as people used to think they would be." But the widespread prevalence of the idea that hell can't be as catastrophically serious as once believed—and as the Bible evidently portrays—is a distinct factor in the modern mood of lightness concerning hell.

A Figure of Speech

"I see hell as a condition that deviates from what we are conditioned for. I definitely think we can experience hell every day and do not think it is deep dark pits. It is any place of disorder, chaos or unrest and I think we take the word too lightly."[3]

These astonishing and paradoxical words came from a businesswoman in the banking industry. They are astonishing in that they reduce hell to nothing more than a figure of speech meaning a poorly organized life. They are paradoxical in that while she asserts that the word is taken too lightly, it is difficult to imagine how the word could be taken any more lightly than she does. One must conclude that if this is hell, then there is no hell at all. For this woman and the significant number who share a similar view, a person's life sort of shifts into hell everytime there's an "out of

---

[3]Ibid.

order'' sign on some aspect of life. But, of course, if things are "gotten together," hell ceases.

Still, this kind of armchair theology doesn't make its appearance with the morning's dew. It can be expressed only in an environment where the awful reality of hell has so drastically eroded that only the slightest suggestion of it remains. True, some of what this woman says is correct. Hell, indeed, is a place of disorder, chaos, and continual unrest. But that's only a minute fraction of hell's complete reality, and this kind of thinking has helped make the darkness of hell merely an off-white. It is impossible to take that kind of hell seriously, because it is no hell at all. It's a condition one Bromo Seltzer can usually cure. Yet, this is the extent to which hell is understood by many moderns.

Ancient Equals Wrong

Our generation has a powerful propensity to believe that what anyone in the past believed to be true is now probably all wrong. Since the church without wavering believed in hell for the full scope of its life, and before that Israel knew of a place of eternal punishment, many today dismiss the whole idea of hell as necessarily erroneous. It's too ancient to be true.

This fallacious line of reasoning often goes, "In the olden days folks couldn't figure out a way to keep bad people and little children in line. So they conjured up the idea of a monstrously grotesque place of gloomy darkness and frightening, everlasting torments. Armed with the threat of consignment to such a terrible place, they scared the stubborn and the young into submission to their cultural patterns."

Such an argument is being widely marketed now in a variety of sizes, shapes, and colors, as it were, and it is one more indicator that hell has lost significance to many moderns.

The case may have been overstated here, but sometimes it takes an overstatement to obtain a balance. Obviously, not all moderns believe that ancient equals wrong. But I have heard words to that effect from more than a few people over the past years. Though only a few carry such a silly idea to its extreme, there are far too many who have persuaded themselves (and others with them) that hell is a concept invented by the ancients that fits nicely into the ignorant life-schemes of antiquity and medieval times. Now with the advent of our marvelous "age of enlightenment," such creations of the past can be shunted to the scrap heap reserved for dilapidated and antiquated ideas and can be replaced by modern, relevant, enlightened, and existential truth (whatever it may be).

The plain, cold-blooded fact is that *most* people today are quite willing to label as offensive anything passed to us from the past as the product of outmoded, naive ignorance—you know, all that ancient stuff like a flat earth, witch burnings, bloodletting, and hell. It's so convenient that there were things in ages past that were wrong, so now we can lump truth offensive to us with whatever was false.

Truth, as we enlightened and informed people of the Age of Aquarius know, cannot be offensive to the educated mind or it is not truth at all. The existentialist thinks, "If it doesn't make me feel good to think about it, of course it's not true." What the ancients called truth is scorned, because they did not possess the "expanded awareness" of the contemporary, educated mind.

Perhaps more people have succumbed to the temptation to make light of hell for this reason than any other. Hell is seen as a nonfunctional antique to be used now only as a decorative piece to spice up a modern, functional home. It's like having great-grandma's spinning wheel in the living room. It's there to look at and to be a conversation piece, but not to use.

It Just Doesn't Exist

There are even those who entertain the pipedream of the nonexistence of hell; they deal with the supposed reality of hell by pompously and boldly ruling out the possibility of its existence. This commonly shows up in two forms: sophisticated and simple. Both make hell nonexistent because *all* life after death is nonexistent.

Some make a "scientific" declaration that when you die,

15

you're dead; and that's all there is to it. You live out your days, short or long, however you choose, and when death's dew lies cold on your brow, it's all over. There is no life after death, no heaven, no hell, no happy hunting ground, no river Styx, no nothing. So why talk about hell? It doesn't exist.

College classrooms and other centers of learning throughout the Western world abound with zealous evangelists for this cause. And pity the poor benighted fool who would dare suggest to the professor that scientific evidences for such a hypothesis are not only weak but totally lacking. Isn't it amazing how easily such an obvious lack of evidence can be so totally glossed over and such confident assertions of the nonexistence of a future life be made by those who style themselves as modern men of science? But the fact that some of the intelligentsia of our day so thoroughly dismiss the idea of hell has contributed greatly to the lightness toward it among the great mass of moderns.

There's also a second, less sophisticated approach to this hypothesis that assumes hell doesn't exist. Those who espouse this premise would never be so bold and blunt as to absolutely assert beyond doubt that everything is over when you die. They say that this is more than likely so. "You see, there are things we don't know, can't know, and won't know. But don't be dismayed; neither be thou worried! Since it is absolutely impossible to know what is on the other side of death (if indeed there's anything), there is obviously nothing now or ever we can do about it."

These agnostics about hell point with glee to the lack of so-called scientific evidence about life after death. And since all knowledge must be supported by scientific evidence, we must remain ignorant on this subject. It's almost as if this assumption itself is a call for laughing and dancing in the streets. The worry is over. Since modern Western man has so committed himself to a theory of knowledge that limits *real* or *sure* knowledge to that which can be demonstrated by the tools of science, he can afford (so he assumes) great luxury in idly or indifferently speculating about those matters that aren't demonstrable in his laboratory and to which he asserts he must ever remain essentially agnostic. It makes no difference that God has plainly revealed truth to us in a nonscientific way. Therefore, live as if hell simply does not exist.

It is important to understand that these five modern theories about hell are just that—modern theories (and groundless theories at that). They certainly don't exhaust all the fantasies about hell that people hold. Yet they do exemplify the prevailing lack of seriousness about it. They should warn us all that something is greatly amiss.

Ancient Ideas about Hell

The shocking current attitudes toward hell are relatively modern phenomena, and they are a cause for great alarm. For thousands of years the word *hell* had the most serious connotations. More than 650 years ago, Dante, the brilliant medieval writer, told in *The Inferno* of the souls he saw and heard in the seventh circle of his multi-layered hell.

> Enormous herds of naked souls I saw,
>   lamenting till their eyes were burned of tears;
>   they seemed condemned by an unequal law,
>
> for some were stretched supine upon the ground,
>   some squatted with their arms about themselves,
>   and others without pause roamed round and round.
>
> Most numerous were those that roamed the plain.
>   Far fewer were the souls stretched on the sand,
>   but moved to louder cries by greater pain.
>
> And over all that sand on which they lay
>   or crouched or roamed, great flakes of flame fell slowly
>   as snow falls in the Alps on a windless day.[4]

Perhaps none other in Dante's time could have written in such a dramatic and artistic fashion, but he was only expressing the

---

[4]Dante, *The Inferno,* John Ciardi, trans. (New York: Mentor, 1954), p. 128.

commonly-held impressions about hell of almost everyone in his world.

Nor did things change much soon thereafter. Three and a half centuries later in yet another literary masterpiece, *Paradise Lost,* John Milton described the fall of Satan and the rebel angels from heaven to hell with these awesome words:

> Him the Almighty Power
> Hurled headlong flaming from the ethereal sky,
> With hideous ruin and combustion, down
> To bottomless perdition; them to dwell
> In adamantine chains and penal fire,
> Who durst defy the Omnipotent to arms.
> Nine times in the space that measures day and night
> To mortal men, he with his horrid crew
> Lay vanquished, rolling in the fiery gulf,
> Confounded, though immortal.[5]

What a contrast these words are to those of the Nashville housewife who in 1978 said, "I don't think it [hell] is a place in the hereafter. The idea of fire and brimstone is a symbolic representation of misery. And misery is being alienated from others and not loved in the sense of worthiness that one feels. . . . Hell is a state of mind, and the only place we experience it is on earth."[6] What a difference a few hundred years can make!

With few exceptions, the first sixteen hundred years of the Christian era witnessed a sober belief in a very real hell that was the place of a very real eternal punishment. Among the ancients the only significant exception to those holding this view was that of Origen, the third-century thinker who was excommunicated by his bishop during his lifetime and anathematized by the Fifth Ecumenical Council after his death.[7] But even he believed there

---

[5]*Paradise Lost* (Chicago: Scott, Foresman and Co., 1898), p. 79, book I, line 44.
[6]*The Nashville Banner,* 22 May 1978, p. 33.
[7]Clement of Alexandria and Gregory of Nyssa are often considered to have had doubts about eternal punishment for the wicked. The case with them, however, is far from conclusive—as will be shown in Chapter 11.

was an actual hell that was a place of divine punishment, though he did not view it as eternal.

It wasn't until the turbulent times of the Protestant Reformation that scattered radicals standing well outside the mainstream of Lutheran, Reformed, and Anglican folds introduced the first challenges to the ancient orthodox view of hell. Though always a small minority, from the sixteenth to the eighteenth centuries they managed to arouse squabbles about hell. But these attacks were from the fringes of Christendom; and even at that, all parties usually agreed there was a literal hell, and the arguments generally centered on the question of the duration of hell. Few, if any, dared suggest that there was no place whatsoever of divine punishment of evildoers for at least some measure of time and to some degree.

However, changes came with the arrival of the nineteenth and twentieth centuries. An avalanche of new ideas about hell descended from many quarters. And this slippage has increased to the point where it is difficult to avoid the impression that there are as many views of hell as there are people willing to consider the subject. So much confusion reigns about hell that every man on the street feels he can be an authority on the subject.

Belief—but Confusion

It's not that people no longer believe there is such a place as hell. Rather, in the deceitful confusion, the idea of hell has lost the dimension of being a serious personal threat. That people still believe in hell is evidenced by a 1977 Iowa Poll.[8] The survey found that most Iowans did, in fact, believe in heaven or hell. But later, in a follow-up poll, the question was asked: "A recent poll showed that most Iowans believe in heaven or hell. In line with this, can you think of anyone you know who might end up in hell?" And, "On a personal basis, how do you think you might end up—in heaven or hell?"

[8]*Des Moines Register,* 25 December 1977, p. 1.

The results of the poll, published in the Christmas Day, 1977, issue of the *Des Moines Register,* showed that sixty-five percent of all Iowans believed they were going to end up in heaven. However, only five percent believed they were going to end up in hell. The other thirty percent were either not sure or had no opinion.

Those twenty-to-one odds against going to hell testify that most Iowans must be saints or that the threat of hell is no longer real to them. After all, which of us is ever in the bottom five percent of anything!

Before we become too comfortable with those odds it should be mentioned that thirty-one percent of all Iowans believed they knew someone else who was going to hell (quite a Christmas present from that thirty-one percent!).

A survey in Minnesota showed almost identical results. According to the *Minneapolis Tribune's* Minnesota Poll, seven out of ten of the state's residents believe in hell. Twenty percent know someone who is a sure bet to go there. Included in that twenty percent are drunk drivers, murderers, and the likes of Idi Amin. On the other hand, this poll revealed that only one in every twenty-five Minnesotans believes he or she deserves to go to hell.[9]

Roman Catholics present a slightly different picture than the general public in Iowa and Minnesota. In an award-winning article, entitled "Hell: Still A Burning Question," author James Brieg quotes the Protestant theologian Martin Marty as saying, "Only one in eight who believe in hell believes it is a threat to him."[10]

Further, Brieg cites a study among Roman Catholics by Father Andrew Greeley that shows although seventy percent of Roman Catholics believe in life after death, only one third of them believe

---

[9]"Only 4% of Minnesotans Feel They're Hellbound," *EP News Service* (25 March 1978), p. 8.

[10]"Hell: Still A Burning Question," *U.S. Catholic* (November 1977), p. 10.

in hell.[11] If these figures are truly representative of Roman Catholics, this would indicate that fewer Roman Catholics than the general public in Minnesota and Iowa believe in hell. But of those who do, more consider it a serious threat than those surveyed in the above-mentioned state polls.

The Plot of the Deceiver

The conclusion these polls force us to accept is twofold. First, the great majority of people still believe in hell. Second, it is *not the existence of hell that is so much in question, but who goes there and why.* Over this second issue there is incredible confusion.

While writing this book, I and the other residents of Santa Barbara, California, were vividly and dramatically reminded of the awesome power of an earthquake. One Sunday afternoon the earth shook steadily for a half minute or so. Walls cracked, dishes poured out of cupboards, supermarket shelves emptied onto floors—the result being millions of dollars worth of damage. It registered at 5.1 on the Richter Scale, a "moderate" earthquake, which was centered in a fault five miles out in the Santa Barbara Channel.

Later, on the same day as the quake in Santa Barbara, I travelled several hundred miles north and stayed in a motel only a mile or two from the infamous San Andreas fault. Understandably, I was far more conscious of the presence of that fault than I had ever been before, even though it was not the one that had caused the Santa Barbara earthquake. The San Andreas fault of course was the culprit for the disastrous San Francisco earthquake in 1906. That fault has demonstrated often its incredible power to move massive chunks of earth.

Now, suppose we deliberately build a great, modern city, skyscrapers and all, somewhere right over that fault (as if San Francisco weren't already there!). Imagine also that we take no

---

[11]Ibid., p. 7.

21

precautions whatever to provide protection against an earthquake. After all, it's been more than seventy years since a city has been demolished by that particular fault. And besides, it was the resulting fire, not the earthquake itself, that did the major damage in San Francisco. So we build our city and live in it giving no serious heed whatever to the possibility of an earthquake. To top it off, we joke about our famous fault and act as if it's not really there.

The rest of the world would rightfully pity us. "Those dumb Californians have duped themselves," people would justifiably say of us.

It is similar with the case of hell. God has spoken and made it emphatically clear in the Bible to Israel of old and to the church of today that a day of judgment is approaching, and eternal punishment in hell is inevitable for those who come under the judgment of God. And yet, people live their lives as though things will continue forever on this earth. But down inside many of them is a pitifully confused fear of what they might face after the inevitability of death. People today need to know what God has spoken about this eternally-important subject.

The purpose of this book is both to demonstrate why the truth of hell has gone out of style in our age and to call us to embrace once again an orthodox and biblical sobriety towards it. That purpose must also include the exhortation to an appropriate suspicion of those who stand against the truth of the reality of hell or treat it lightly. They are indeed among mankind's greatest enemies.

To achieve this purpose, it will first be necessary to carefully evaluate the staggering effect this "grayness" about the darkness of hell has already had on us both in terms of the moral and spiritual bankruptcy in our culture and in our experience of God. The major reasons why hell has gone out of style will then be thoroughly displayed, which will enable us to get a picture of what has caused this erosion of truth about hell.

We must also examine the faith of the historic church throughout the centuries. And, of course, the teaching of the Scriptures, both Old and New Testaments, will be set forth in order to remove any vestige of confusion.

Finally, we will conclude with a statement of hope—God's way for human beings to be confident of their eternal state, including a sketch of the blessings in store for those who experience true entrance into the kingdom of God.

2
The Cost of Being Gray_____

> . . . I pray thee therefore, father, that thou wouldest send him
> [Lazarus] to my father's house: For I have five brethren; that he
> may testify unto them, lest they also come into this place of torment
> (Luke 16:27,28; KJV).

Thus spoke the rich man to Abraham in the parable told by
Jesus. Was it that the man's five brothers had not been warned?
No, for Abraham had said, ". . . 'They have Moses and the
Prophets; let them hear them' " (Luke 16:29). The rich man, knowing that his brothers, like himself, had lost the concept of the
reality of eternal punishment, pled: ". . . 'Father Abraham, but if
someone goes to them from the dead, they will repent!' " (v. 30).
There is a warning for our age in the awful finality of Abraham's
reply: ". . . 'If they do not listen to Moses and the Prophets,
neither will they be persuaded if someone rises from the dead.' "

At the very root of disbelief in the eternal punishment of the
wicked is a questioning of the truthfulness of God. Obviously, the
rich man (and his brothers) did not believe God was telling the
truth about hell, and neither does the unbelieving world today—
including some Christians. When men lack that confidence in
God, when they have persuaded themselves that He will not do
what He says He will do, they feel free to go their own way. The
result is eternal loss. As Pieper said, "The purpose of this shocking doctrine of eternal damnation is to warn against unbelief and
carnal security and thus to save from eternal damnation."[1]

---
[1]*Christian Dogmatics,* vol. 3 (St. Louis: Concordia, 1950-53), p. 540

Closely related to eternal punishment is eternal redemption. The atonement Christ made is infinite, because it was God who suffered and died in Christ. An infinite atonement was necessary because man's sin, being against the most Holy God, is an infinite offense. The enormity of that offense is demonstrated by the fact that it deserves eternal punishment. Moreover, the scriptural and traditional teaching on the redemption simply assumes the validity of retributive punishment on the part of God. If we lose sight of the fact that the wicked deserve punishment, the redemption is utterly pointless and nonexistent.

Grayness and the Gospel

Grayness, that is, being in a noncommittal fog about eternal punishment, causes us first of all to undervalue the gospel itself. Matthew Horberry, writing in the mid-eighteenth century, saw the problem clearly:

> The great Argument for working out our Salvation in the present Life while it is called today, is because the night cometh, when no Man can work. But if Men were once taught to believe that there will be another Day, that will answer their purpose as well; it is natural to think, that they will be too apt to trust to that Resource, and so to live and die without Repentance. I don't say that this Conduct would be reasonable, but that it is likely to be Fact, considering how strongly Men are attached to their old and favourite Sins.[2]

If there is nothing to escape from, if the notion of such a judgment is optional, if there is no imminent danger for those who do not walk with God, then where is the value and worth of the gospel of Christ and His kingdom? What is the difference between the kingdom of light and the kingdom of darkness?

Let confusion reign about hell and we slide into the gray, foggy mist in which light and darkness are indistinguishable, and the things of this world begin to seem as important as the gospel of

---

[2]*An Enquiry into the Scripture Doctrine Concerning the Duration of Future Punishment* (London: n.p., 1744), pp. 294-95.

Christ. Material goods, financial security, and a comprehensive medical policy begin to seem more likely to care for our needs than a vague "salvation from what?" Contributions to the United Fund and the Red Cross seem more apt to relieve the total distress of the poor than the proclamation of pie-in-the-sky, by and by.

All the gusto we can get in our one-time around begins to make more sense than some ascetic denial of our appetites when we may, and probably will, all get the same treatment in the end. The ability to plumb the secrets of micro-universes and uncover the activities of stars that are light-years away seems equally intriguing as exploring union and communion with God. His Word becomes so ambiguous that no one knows for sure what it means when it says, "Who shall be punished with everlasting destruction from the presence of the Lord, and from the glory of His power" (2 Thess. 1:9, KJV).

The Attitude of Ingratitude

Moreover, the grayness drives away gratitude. The Christian who has lost sight of his being delivered from eternal punishment will not rise up in praise and thanksgiving to God for His majesty, mercy, goodness, and grace. No, forgetting the misery we deserve and thus forgetting that we are spared from it by His grace alone, we find words of praise dusty on our lips. Songs about the New Jerusalem, that city where there is no suffering, sorrow, pain, or tears, are meaningless because we do not believe in everlasting hopelessness. To complicate things even more, that attitude of ingratitude is contagious. People everywhere sense it and catch it. The disease becomes an epidemic.

When grayness comes upon our hearts, we lose the proper gratitude for the coming of the eternal Son of God in the flesh, the most astounding occurrence of all time or eternity. Does any one of us really think that sin is just a debt we couldn't pay and God could freely forgive us just by *saying* so? If that were true, the birth, life, death, and resurrection of our Savior, with His sufferings and persecutions, would have all been a mistake.

Christian, sin is a terribly real debt, an incredible offense towards God. The kindness of God cannot gloss over your disobedience. Justice has to be done. God is not just benevolent, He is also just; and God's justice was fully satisfied when God the Son suffered on our behalf. Accepting Him and His costly vicarious atonement becomes mere meaningless form to souls who have no sense of eternal damnation. And where the sense of deliverance from unending torment is lost, the tables turn and men feel they've done Christ a favor by receiving Him.

Indeed, if we must speak grayly of that which is to come, if we cannot draw a line that cleaves clearly between life and death, if we cannot positively picture light here and darkness there, then sinful men cannot be awakened to their own personal guilt and danger. They lose the opportunity to experience the misery that is their actual condition. Such people are prone to wander from Christ. They are cheated of the holy soul-searching dread of divine punishment. But if such a passionate fear excites people, they will run from the wrath to come, flee to Christ and His church, and sell all to lay hold of God as revealed in the gospel.

That's right! When the church gets bound up in the misty confusion of the reasoning of the age, it no longer serves effectively as the instrument of God to reach out to sinners and snatch them from eternal destruction. When His own people begin to buy the worldly idea that retributive punishment is a totally wrong and repulsive idea—that the only possible value of punishment is to teach, reform, or deter; when His own accept the view that eternal damnation is the grossly unjust penalty to pay for the piddling sins of men; when they become convinced that hell isn't nearly so bad as the Scriptures "seem" to say; when they can't bear to think of being in heaven when all these "good people" are in hell; when God's own are moved by the groundless argument that He is defeated if just one single soul, or even the devil himself, is finally lost; then they have departed from the truth, deprived themselves of His good government, and forfeited their place in God's purpose.[3]

Grayness and Godliness

Oh, but isn't that a very extreme statement? Not at all; it's the truth, for that fuzzy, gray thinking about hell does bad things to the children of God. It deters them from holiness. They cease caring how they live. No longer are they afraid of returning to sin and folly;[4] no longer do they refrain from the indulgence of the various temptations that cross their paths. The fear and reverence of the Lord is lost, and that is an unspeakable loss.

Is this not precisely what is happening among the people of God today? Godliness is out; divorce, the murder of unborn children, and sexual self-indulgence are in. Even those who style themselves as evangelical, conservative, and fundamental tolerate such evils in their churches.

Why this indifference? It's the grayness gained from the loss of the reality of divine warnings against such things. ". . . I forewarn you just as I have forewarned you that those who practice such things shall not inherit the kingdom of God" (Gal. 5:21).

What does grayness on eternal judgment do to you, personally? What does it mean when you assimilate the world's god (not the real God, as the Scriptures describe Him and the church has known Him) who is all benevolence and mushy love, without holiness and justice?

Let's take an example: the discipline of our children. Con-

---

[3]Cf. C. S. Lewis, *The Problem of Pain* (London: Macmillan, 1944), especially Chapter 8.

[4]There is no authentic replacement for the word *folly* here. The dictionary reads:*folly,* n., 1: lack of good sense or normal prudence and foresight, 2: a foolish act or idea, 3(a): *evil wickedness* [emphasis mine], especially lewd behavior, (b): criminally or tragically foolish actions or conduct, 4: an excessively costly or unprofitable undertaking.

sciously or unconsciously, when we begin to operate by the idea that if the God of the universe is all benevolence and why should any of His creatures (parents) be less, we let things slide and pass. We exert no authority in the lives of our children, and soon we have no authority. Neglecting the admonition, "The rod and reproof give wisdom: but a child left to himself bringeth his mother to shame" (Prov. 29:15, KJV), we deprive them of the experience of living in a proper home and thus fail to give them a foundation for appreciating the lordship of Christ.

There is far more. If the issues of heaven and hell are gray, matters of right and wrong also become gray. If there is someone where you work who is attractive, and a sense of affinity grows, and pleasure and desire rise when you look at each other, and you just *know* that it would be right, and your husband or wife does not need to know, adultery comes easily. Moral codes change suddenly, even without thinking about it. Your new code becomes that of the world around you, but your greatest fears and guilts come when you violate the true code. Saint John Chrysostom, the eloquent and godly bishop of the fourth and fifth centuries, had a warning about that:

> Beloved, we need great diligence in all things, for we shall render account of and undergo a strict enquiry both of words and works . . . "For we must all appear before the judgment-seat of Christ, that each one may be recompensed for his deeds in the body, according to what he has done, whether good or bad" (2 Cor. 5:10). Let us ever bear in mind this tribunal that we may thus be enabled at all times to continue in virtue; for as he who has cast out from his soul that day, rushes like a horse that has burst his bridle to precipices . . . so he that always retains this fear will walk soberly.[5]

Grayness and the Christian's Perspective

As this grayness reaches into our relationships with people, it causes a blurring of the distinction between those who are the

---

[5]*Homilies on St. John*, homily 39 (John 5:23 ff.).

people of God and those who are not. For, if everyone is eventually to be saved or to have the same fate, then what unique reality is there in "union with Christ"? If you do not consciously entertain such a union, those outside the church begin to seem to be models and companions just as appropriate as those in the church. Having lost the consciousness of the kingdoms of life and death as separate entities with different lords and nonoverlapping subjects, it becomes just as easy to feel at home with the one as with the other.

Further, grayness causes a loss of urgency about the people you love and live with who need salvation and the lordship of Christ. It may even encourage them to have a false sense of security. A man begins to think, "If hell might not be real, I don't have to worry about that; and if hell might not be real, heaven might not be real. I can take my chances." Next come the jokes about hell. That's why people laughingly say, "Oh, go to hell," and "I want to go to hell, because that's where all my friends will be," and "If hell were real, I'd be there by now!"

Joking about this matter that is no joking matter, men run further and further from God. There is no fear of doing wrong because the conscience has been blunted. There is no inner pain of remorse felt as a preview of that ultimate, intense, and everlasting pain that is to come. When a man has fooled himself into believing that we all ultimately share the same fate, why on earth will he want redemption? He won't.

I cannot tell about other ages, other times, other lands. But I can tell you about our nation in our time. Having forgotten hell, it feels it can afford to forget God. Having forgotten God, it has forgotten His kingdom; it builds its own, which is not its own, but Satan's.

And so we live in a brave new world where there is greater and greater pressure for indulgent benevolence, greater and greater pressure to allow anyone to do anything he wants—"as long as it doesn't hurt anyone else" (with "hurt anyone else" being more and more vaguely defined). Homosexuality becomes an appropriate "alternate life-style." Adultery suddenly is good, not bad. Divorce and abandonment of children are the best thing if an adult's "fulfillment" is at stake. It's right to overcharge the poor if a "decent profit" is in jeopardy. War is wrong if *I* will get hurt; but if *I* think it is a righteous cause, then it's good. Stealing is right if it's done by (or from) a big, impersonal company. My father and my mother did such a poor job of rearing me and thus ruined my life; let them go off to a nursing home—a cheap one—and send me their money, for *I* deserve it.

Yes, there is a difference in a society that has lost sight of the everlasting punishment for the wicked. Grayness in that area brings increasing moral grayness with it. Sadly, our society is not the best the world has ever known, and our morals are not the highest ever seen. They border on being the worst.

Grayness and the Eternal Damnation of Men

But a decaying society and moral filth are not the most tragic parts of all. Men and women are going to hell and that is the gravest, most serious consequence of grayness. Take care, "Christian America!" Take care, wise and outstanding sinners! Be careful about the evil temptations and horrible examples you are setting before your children and your peers! Be careful how you spread your infectious grayness to others by your demonstrations of how delightful your freedoms are! Watch out when you pass a law making evil the right thing to do! Watch out when you confidently write books and articles saying that your ungodly and wicked opinions are true! Watch out when you persecute the poor and the godly for the sake of your "conscience"!

It just might be that the evil consequences of your wicked deeds will range from generation to generation among your descendants, bringing judgment upon judgment, long after you are dead! It just might be that you yourself, impossible as the thought is to you, may end up in the devil's hell for all eternity. For many, the cost of grayness about hell will be the darkness of hell itself.

3
Hell and the Humanists _____

As I have briefly indicated, hell's going out of style is decidedly a modern phenomenon. The record is clear. There are four fundamental reasons why hell has been air-conditioned or denied by modern critics: (1) the rise of humanistic thought, (2) the doctrine of universalism, (3) higher criticism and impugning of the Scriptures, and (4) the secularization of public education. This and the ensuing three chapters deal with each of these matters separately.

*   *   *   *   *

Hell was thoroughly and firmly in style in Christendom for nineteen of our twenty Christian centuries. This is not to say there were no challenges whatsoever to the doctrine of eternal punishment. But challenges were for the most part limited to small schismatic or heretical sects, and these were all met fiercely and successfully by the church. The Socinians of the seventeenth century, for example, (see Chapter 11) angrily attacked the doctrine of eternal punishment. The church responded with a powerful and triumphant counterattack. When the smoke and dust of the battle had settled, the Socinian influence in the church of that day was negligible.

Thorny Theologians
It's only in the twentieth century that the doctrine of hell has begun to wane enough that it can be suggested it is going out of vogue.

That it has faded in our own time, and increasingly so at that, cannot be denied. Egged on by a marked measure of victory, the enemies of the orthodox doctrine of eternal punishment have stepped up the intensity and scope of their attacks. The church must once again rise to this challenge as it always has before. We must sharpen our wits and prepare for battle. To do that, we first must grasp the basic reasons why hell is no longer popular.

A simple one-sentence answer cannot adequately explain why hell has been forgotten. This tragic, soul-devastating loss has a number of causes—causes that are both complex and revealing.

The schemes of the avowed enemies of the truly orthodox doctrine of eternal punishment are many. But their intention remains the same: to banish from the church every vestige of the doctrine of eternal punishment as it is presented in Scripture and as it has been comprehended by the church of God for more than nineteen hundred years.

Consider the following statement from John A.T. Robinson, the Bishop of Woolich no less, in which he feigns the case on hell as already settled:

> There are still a few who would like to bring back hell, as some want to bring back birching and hanging. They are usually the same types who wish to purge Britain of horror comics, sex, and violence.[1]

This heretical bishop would lead his readers to believe that no one any longer believes there is a hell! The idea of hell falls into the same category as floggings and hangings, and anyone believing hell should be brought back into its proper historic focus is some kind of nut. The bishop is in error on all counts, and he knows it. In addition, he seems to be advocating horror comics, sex, and violence for Great Britain. I am amazed a bishop would countenance such things for his people!

I'll concede that Robinson is an ultra-extremist who feeds on sensationalism, but he is not alone in making such presumptuous

---

[1]*But That I Can't Believe* (New York: The New American Library, 1967), p. 69.

assertions. The highly respected European theologian, Emil Brunner, wrote:

> . . . That is the revealed will of God and the plan for the world which He discloses, a plan of universal salvation, of gathering all things into Christ. We hear not one word in the Bible of a dual plan, a plan of salvation and its polar opposite. The will of God has but one point, it is unambiguous and positive. It has one aim, not two.[2]

It may be a clever ploy to insinuate as Brunner does that orthodoxy has perverted the true biblical teaching. But it's neither honest in method nor true to the facts. It's nothing more than a "cheap shot" emotionalism to imply that the church's traditional understanding of Scripture on this issue of hell is foolish, misguided, and contrary to the will of God.

About one thing, however, Brunner is correct: The will of God is positive and unambiguous. Positively, there is an eternal heaven, and unambiguously, there is an eternal hell—all emotionally grounded contradictions notwithstanding. The reality of truth cannot be altered by "gimmicky theology," no matter how ingenious it might appear.

The Root of the Modern Problem

All scholars who have studied thoroughly the full history of the doctrine of eternal punishment are agreed that challenges to the doctrine have occurred from the sixteenth century and on. As already noted, Origen, who died A.D. 254, and who was later condemned by two ecumenical councils, was the only significant ancient who actually challenged this doctrine. Then, among the notable medieval theologians, only the scholastic John Scotus Erigena had a significantly different treatment of the doctrine of hell. His scheme was little more than a reworking of Origen's.

So, with the overwhelming weight of over sixteen hundred years on its side, what was responsible for the sudden and dra-

---

[2]*Eternal Hope* (Philadelphia: Westminster Press, 1954), p. 182.

matic upsurge in challenges and denunciations of the historic doctrine of hell?

Humanism is a most accurate one-word answer to this question. Until the dawn of the Renaissance, the men and women of the Christian era saw the universe and mankind revolving about God. But with the rebirth of ancient, classical learning in the fifteenth and sixteenth centuries came a subtle, yet mammoth, shift in man's status relative both to the universe and to God. Under the label of humanism, this man-creature, created in the image of God, was exalted to a position he had never before known—even at the hands of the ancient Greek philosophers. Man, with his marvelous capacities and capabilities, was elevated to new and dizzy heights. For the humanist who pursued this course, man became the focal point of the universe. All else revolved about him.

This humanistic philosophy did not totally replace God; it *displaced* Him. Man was encouraged to invade territory hitherto reserved for God alone. The pattern was set: In humanism man moves up and in, while God drops down and out.

Every nook and cranny of Western life and experience was permeated by the influence of Renaissance humanism, and the entire course of Western thought and practice has been altered since then. That influence has, in fact, been augmented rather than diminished in the modern era. Our own age is still very much the child of the Renaissance as is evident by the current all-prevailing humanistic orientation to life and thought.

Once committed to the philosophy of humanism, a theologian must undertake complete revamping of all orthodox Christian doctrine. From his lofty new perch, man must reinterpret himself, his purpose, and his destiny. Thus theology has received "general repairs" from humanism, but the doctrine of eternal punishment in particular has been singled out for a major overhaul.

From the sixteenth century on, God's judgment was a constant target for attack by humanists both within and outside the church. Hell and humanism didn't mix; they can't mix and never will mix. It just won't do to have highly exalted man experiencing the torments of hell eternally. First, it is presumed that the precious creature couldn't possibly do anything bad enough to warrant such punishment. And even more significantly, the humanists are convinced that God could not bear the eternal loss of even one of these marvelous man-creatures.

The humanist theologian Bishop Robinson pronounces:

> Christ, in Origen's old words, remains on the Cross as long as one sinner remains in hell. That is not a speculation; it is a statement grounded in the very necessity of God's nature. In a universe of love, there can be no heaven which tolerates a chamber of horrors, no hell for any which does not at the same time make it hell for God. He cannot endure that—for that would be the final mockery of His nature—and He will not.[3]

You've got to hand it to the bishop. He's got a way with words and sounds almost convincing. You will notice that he has God adjusting His existence according to man, not vice versa. This is the perfect representation of the humanist's thinking with his all-sovereign man served by an ever-devoted God.

Who says God's nature can't endure the reality of eternal punishment for the wicked? Jesus Christ surely didn't. He didn't even come close. It was He who spoke of Gehenna "where their worm does not die, and the fire is not quenched" (Mark 9:48). Again, speaking of the day He would judge all men, he said: " 'Then He [Jesus Christ] will answer them, saying, "Truly I say to you, to the extent that you did not do it to one of the least of these, you did not do it to Me." And these will go away into eternal punishment, but the righteous into eternal life' " (Matt. 25:45,46). That doesn't sound as though Christ is still on the cross!

---

[3]"Universalism—Is It Heretical?" *Scottish Journal of Theology* (June 1949), p. 155.

We really must take our pick: the humanists, such as Robinson, or the Lord Jesus Christ. We can't have them both. They are as far apart as heaven and hell. It is not man's prerogative to decide what God is permitted to do with him. It is God's prerogative to determine man's eternal state. That He has done and that He will do.

The humanists have evolved a God who is nothing more than a tired old man who would need an eternal supply of Kleenex to daub His everlasting eyes should one of these God-denying, humanity-hating, blaspheming, self-centered, self-seeking, murderous, rebellious man-creatures remain outside the realm of the blessedness of His heaven. Fortunately, for all of us, most human judges, even the worst of them, aren't that irresponsible and indulgent. Could it be that the humanist has created a God in his own image and to his own liking in order to hedge his bet against the whole idea of any divine retribution? If so, he will have to work harder to thoroughly persuade himself—let alone the rest of a God-conscious world.

Humanism and Punishment

Armed with the erroneous conviction that man is basically good from head to toe, humanism has produced a totally revised and false understanding of punishment. Retributive punishment, punishment that is the accepted payment for an offense, is considered by the humanist to be neither necessary nor proper for man's heart, which is now no longer ". . . more deceitful than all else . . . desperately sick . . ." (Jer. 17:9). Therefore, if God is to be allowed to punish man at all, His punishment must be limited to corrective and educational purposes only. Out of this novel idea has evolved the modern theory subscribed to by so many that fear of punishment is not a true deterrent to bad behavior.

The notion, of course, is absurd. Whoever heard of a successful society without appropriate punishments for lawbreakers? Naturally, those who have a quarrel with the idea of proper conduct will do what they can to remove any and all barriers to bad behavior. I wonder how many Americans would have their income tax returns in by April 15 if there were no penalties for failure to do so? Even good citizens might inadvertently let that date slip by unnoticed. The fact is, there is a deadline, and there is a penalty for failing to meet it.

The almighty, sovereign God who created man has made some demands on His creature; and He has every right to make whatever demands He chooses. The matter isn't open to question, and there are penalties for failure to meet His demands. There is retribution. The ultimate penalty for not satisfying God's demands is eternal torment in hell.

Now, one can say he doesn't believe it or that it's not so. He can even get audacious and declare he could never believe in a God such as that. But what we say or believe about God and whether or not he should punish men for evil doesn't in actuality make the slightest bit of difference.

God's enemies can whine about how severe it all sounds saying that "a loving God just couldn't do such a thing as send some human being to a place of frightful eternal punishment." But nothing changes with God. Even if God were a vicious tyrant, and He's not, such whimpering would not make the most minute particle of difference. Those with such ideas may become really "uppity" and say, "Well, if that's the kind of God He is, I'd rather go to hell than be with Him!" Still, they alter nothing—though, sadly, they may get their heart's desire, a wish they'll greatly regret having had.

Thus, theories that tamper with the historic doctrine of hell or those that seek to diminish its seriousness are nothing more than exercises in sound and fury; they signify nothing—at least so far as changing the truth of God. These exercises may, however, have disastrous eternal effects on the people who hear them—similar to the drunk who is assured that alcohol is really nothing but a very profitable factor in improving his lot in life.

Centuries of human experience do not indicate that man needs any more encouragement to do evil. But that is exactly what is accomplished by those who push the "no-hell" ideology. Their net effect in modern times has been to lull too many people to sleep. How agonizing it will be for these who sleep to awaken to the "weeping and wailing and gnashing of teeth."

4
Universalism: The Impossible Dream _____

Humanism, universalism, modern biblical criticism, and the secularization of public education are, as I have said, four major culprits in the open warfare occurring in our culture against God's prerogative of punishment.

Foundational to all four is the tacit assumption that the historic church has *always* been in error in its understanding of God and eternity. Each proposes to exchange that ancient and tried understanding with a modern substitute. But these cut-rate replacements won't pass for the "original equipment" they seek to succeed. Neither will they survive the test of time and truth nor the ability to speak successfully to human experience. They must be exposed and rejected.

The Granddaddy of False Hopes

Universalism, the second contributive reason for the "disappearance" of hell, is the label applied to those varieties of religious theories stating that all men will ultimately be saved. It's important to arrive at a clear definition of this term. Some erroneously believe that all universalists teach that there is no punishment of any kind for the ungodly. This is not necessarily so. Many universalists believe there is a temporary punishment for the reprobate. But universalists always insist that all men will ultimately enjoy the eternal bliss of heaven.

Universalism has been a gigantic factor in the modern decline of hell. Infecting virtually every area of human endeavor, the offerings of the universalists are so tempting to the sorely tempted. One has to admit that it would sound like music to the convicted, unrepentent murderer's ears were he to hear that there was, after all, no serious penalty for murder, and that his crime was just a mistake and everything would be straightened out shortly. That's the appeal of universalism to the world. This hell thing is wrong, needless, peripheral, or at least ultimately inconsequential. Everything is going to be fine. At least that's the line the universalists promote.

Universalism travelled a bumpy, unfriendly road for many centuries. (A brief history of universalism is presented in Chapter 11.) Being so obviously contrary to the doctrine of the Bible and the church, it's minute number of adherents in antiquity made little progress. The Renaissance propelled the multiplication of universalists into the sixteenth, seventeenth, and eighteenth centuries. But even with this increase, the influence of universalism was generally limited to a very small sphere almost always sealed off from the church at large.

The story of the past two centuries, however, is different. Boosted on by the ever-growing wave of humanism, universalism has gained an ascendency that universalists never dreamed possible even one hundred years ago. It took a long time to get the ball rolling, but once it got in motion, momentum has steadily gained until universalism has become a powerful force in our time.

Support for Universalism: A Twofold Speculation

At rock bottom, the doctrine of universalism is a speculative philosophical system. Universalists do not begin with either the biblical material on the subject of eternal punishment or with the historic church's interpretation of that data. Instead, they start with two philosophical assumptions born in their own imaginations.

The first is that God's love is so perfectly good and perfectly sovereign that there is no way it could suffer the defeat of allow-ing one of His creatures to end up being eternally punished. That would mean, they contend, that there is something more powerful than the love of God. The second assumption has to do with the free will of man. Stripped of all the fancy philosophical language, it boils down to the argument that if man stands at a crossroads with only two options, one leading to heaven and the other leading to eternal torment, he doesn't really have free will at all. He is *forced* to choose one or the other. How, they contend, under such pressure could free will truly be exercised? According to D. P. Walker, a contemporary writer whose book, *The Decline of Hell,* favors universalism, these two assumptions stretch all the way back to Origen:

> The whole of Origen's eschatology is based on two principles: first, the justice and goodness of an omnipotent Creator; secondly, the absolute free will of every rational being (man, animated star, angel, demon).[1]

At first glance those two postulates the universalists pull out of thin air seem impressive. But if you think about them for a few minutes, they disappear into the vapor from which they came.

Who says the love of God is defeated if any created being ends up in torment? The universalists do, but God doesn't. The whole sham is based on the presumption that man, not God, decides what the love of God is all about. Besides, if you want to look at it philosophically, it is equally plausible and legitimate to postulate that the love of God cannot be perfectly sovereign unless the rebellious and reprobate are forever punished. The fact is, when it comes to the subject of eternal hell, we aren't interested in philosophical speculations one way or the other. We are concerned only with the truth of God. It has been spoken, and it is not in doubt.

The universalists claim they possess the truth. Those who

---

[1]*The Decline of Hell* (London: Rontledge and Kegan Paul, 1964), p. 12.

believe there is a place of eternal torment claim they have the truth. Who is right? Is there a way to be sure?

The *safest,* most *sure* way to learn the truth of God is to discover what the overwhelming consensus of the church has been with respect to what God says in the Scriptures on the subject over the nearly two thousand years of history. Anyone who examines the facts will know that the church has always agreed the Scriptures teach that God is perfectly good and perfectly sovereign, and that He assigns the wicked to eternal punishment. All the wishful speculations to the contrary do not alter that one jot or tittle.

Do you remember when as a kid you got something for Christmas that was very expensive, but it wasn't what you wanted—like a new suit when you wanted a baseball and bat? All the wishing in the world for the sports equipment couldn't transform the suit. So it is with the universalists. They want Christmas to remove the threat of hell from everyone, even from those who don't want to receive *God's* Christmas gift—Jesus Christ—to this race.

Or about that second assumption, the one that says man doesn't really have free will if he's offered only two narrow choices. A child can see through that one!

Living just a mile from the Santa Barbara airport, I can hear those United and Air West jets landing throughout the day. Now suppose one of those pilots feels there is an infringement on his free will because he must use that silly little old runway. So he decides to land on my street. That's free will? That's suicide and homicide! The pilot does exercise free will every time he lands. He can use the runway or he can pass over. If he's going to land in Santa Barbara, he's *got* to use that runway. But if he attempts to exercise his free will by putting a 727 down on my street, both his free will and mine will come to an abrupt end. Free will is not hindered by limited options or pressure. It is actually enhanced because it is called into realistic service.

Who decides what free will is: creature or Creator? Or who decides what free will can do: creature or Creator? God, not man, determines the extent and content of free will. In this matter of eternity there are two choices. That's it—whether we like it or not.

In a discussion such as this, two Scripture verses keep coming to my mind: "On the contrary, who are you, O man, who answers back to God? The thing molded will not say to the molder, 'Why did you make me like this,' will it? Or does not the potter have a right over the clay . . ." (Rom. 9:20,21). You see, we're right back to this humanism thing again. That's why universalism is so much bigger on this side of the Renaissance than it was on the other. Man has gotten too big for his britches. He now presumes to tell God how it is that He must have made him, and that has to be roughly equal to God Himself, or at the very least, not more than a hair's breadth below.

In the light of the Scriptures and the church's teaching on them, universalism falls flat on its face. It operates from philosophical presuppositions about God and man that aren't true. If you grant the universalist those presuppositions, he's got a good argument. But if you insist on the truth, the dream of universalism turns into a nightmare.

The Church Rejects Universalism

Some may be asking, "What's this business you mention about the Scriptures *and* the overwhelming consensus of the church's interpretation of them and what they teach about eternal punishment? Aren't the Scriptures themselves enough?" The problem here is not with the Scriptures. They are in no way lacking. But there are serious problems with the interpretation of those Scriptures. As I will show shortly, many universalists also claim the support of the Scriptures.

What I said was that the *safest,* most *sure* path to the truth of God is to test what the overwhelming consensus of the church has been regarding the interpretation of those Scriptures. John Wesley, the illustrious founder of Methodism, in his more mature years advocated the following rule for interpreting Scripture: *"Consensus veterum quod ad omnibus quod ubique quod semper creditum,"* which loosely translated is, "The consensus of the ancients which has been believed by everyone, everywhere and always."[2]

Individual and private interpretation of Scripture will never do on any issue, including hell. The overwhelming consensus of the church is not infallible in the sense of Scripture, but it is infinitely safer than anyone's private interpretation taken as the guide to truth. There's too much room to be wrong and too much room for debate. Even when we're correct, our own interpretations lack *authority.* Everyone may justifiably disagree at will.

Giving in to the authority of personal, private interpretation of Scripture without the consensus of the whole church promotes at least two evil ends. First, there is a denial of the validity and reality of the Holy Spirit's work. He has never retired from working in the church in the past two thousand years. Secondly, many a universalist settles securely into his error by privately interpreting Scripture to back his position. He will sink himself, and he just may take many others down with him into the very depths of hell. The private conviction that Scripture teaches eternal punishment will never be adequate to authoritatively put down this horrendous error. As always, it takes the strong united voice of the church to check and correct heresy.

Supposed Biblical Support for Universalism

It is amazing to many Christians that many universalists maintain that the Scriptures teach universalism. These universalists are as persuaded of this as are those who, Bible in hand, attempt to prove the opposite.

Six Scripture passages are invariably appealed to by the uni-

---

[2]*John Wesley,* ed. Albert Outler (New York: Oxford Univ. Press, 1964). Taken from John Wesley's Journal, January 24, 1738. (The translation is mine.)

versalists in support of their contention that all men will ultimately be saved. Let's look at them.

1. " 'And I, if I be lifted up from the earth, will draw all men to Myself' " (John 12:32).

2. "So then as through one transgression there resulted condemnation to all men, even so through one act of righteousness there resulted justification of life to all men" (Rom. 5:18).

3. "And that he may send Jesus, the Christ appointed for you, whom heaven must receive until the period of restoration of all things about which God spoke by the mouth of His holy prophets from ancient time" (Acts 3:20,21).

4. "He [God] made known to us the mystery of His will, according to His kind intention which He purposed in Him with a view of an administration suitable to the fulness of the times, that is, the summing up of all things in Christ, things in the heavens and things upon the earth . . ." (Eph. 1:9,10).

5. "For as in Adam all die, so also in Christ all shall be made alive. But each in his own order: Christ the first fruits, after that those who are Christ's at His coming, then comes the end, when He delivers up the kingdom to the God and Father, when He has abolished all rule and all authority and power. For He must reign until He has put all His enemies under His feet. The last enemy that will be abolished is death. For He has put all things in subjection under His feet. But when He says, 'All things are put in subjection,' it is evident that He is excepted who put all things in subjection to Him. And when all things are subjected to Him, then the Son Himself also will be subjected to the One who subjected all things to Him, that God may be all in all" (1 Cor. 15:22-28).

6. "Therefore also God highly exalted Him, and bestowed on Him the name which is above every name, that at the name of Jesus every knee should bow, of those who are in heaven, and on earth, and under the earth, and that every tongue should confess

that Jesus Christ is Lord, to the glory of God the Father'' (Phil. 2:9-11).

Other Scriptures are sometimes added to these to support the idea of ultimate salvation for all men.[3] But the above six passages are the universalist's mainstays.

If these were the only Scriptures on the subject, universalism might have a case. Unfortunately for the universalists, these are but a handful of those that bear on the subject of eternal punishment. In fact, there are so many more that, rather than list them here, I will devote considerable space later to dealing with them in detail.

If someone says to the universalist, "Oh, those verses don't teach universalism. Why there is an explanation for each one of them. The plain teaching of Scripture is against this whole heretical idea," he will likely retort, "Says *you*. You twist the Scriptures to your own ends. Those Scriptures irrefutably teach the ultimate salvation of all.''

So goes the war of recent centuries. Personally, I agree completely with the first speaker's statement and heartily reject the second's. But this doesn't win the battle except for those of us who have already decided what we believe Scripture teaches. Obviously, this leaves out an awesome number of people who must not be left to think that this is just a matter of one interpretation against another.

There is, however, one argument that no universalist can gainsay. Let me repeat it here for emphasis.

The historic church has unequivocally, emphatically, and continually endorsed the view that the "all" in those Scriptures refers to *all who believe*. They do not teach universalism and never have. The Scriptures do indeed declare the eternal punish-

---

[3] Cf. 1 Timothy 2:4; 2 Peter 3:9; 2 Corinthians 5:19; Colossians 1:20; Titus 2:11; Hebrews 2:9; and 1 John 2:2.

ment of the wicked. There can be no argument over that point. Only a fool would say that God will one day holler, "Ali-ali oxen free," and everyone—including the purposefully wicked—will come scampering in.

We may argue all we want about what we personally believe Scripture teaches. There is surely legitimacy and profit in that. But we dare not stop there. The full weight of the church must be brought to bear. There is nothing wrong with being convinced that we're right according to the Scriptures. Something's dreadfully wrong if we're not. Yet our conviction of rightness has little to do with proving to others that we're right. On the other hand, when we have the overpowering weight of the consensus of the church's testimony of Scripture behind our doctrine, we have the *safest* and *surest* testimony possible; and the witness to truth is far greater.

In saying this, I do not believe for a moment that this argument pits the church against the Scriptures for supremacy of authority, or that the church vies with the Scriptures as the ledger for truth. Neither is remotely the case. The finality of Scripture is not called into question here. But I'll happily state that this argument does pit the church's corporate interpretation of Scripture against the free-lance opinion of any one individual. Only the arrogant, unrepentant, and unsubmissive will argue for the authority of individual interpretation over that of the Holy Spirit in the church. Far too much room has been granted for private interpretation of Scripture, particularly in contemporary Protestantism. That thoughtless latitude is made to order for the universalist; he's more than happy to rest his case on such a foundation.

Two Hitchhikers To Universalism

Two "subschemes" universalism has spawned, conditionalism and annihilation, need to be mentioned in passing because of the accompanying role they have played with universalism in the progressive decline in the belief in hell.

48

As universalism slowly gained prominence, there were those who wanted to be universalists but just couldn't bring themselves to justify it. Agreeing with universalists in rejecting future punishment for the wicked, they couldn't quite swallow the notion that all men will ultimately be saved. This led to the creation of some variations, conditionalism and annihilationism, as attractive options. These doctrinal "first-cousins" to universalism differ in that they allow for an eternal state of bliss and blessing for some but eternal punishment and torment for none.

Conditionalists believe that human beings are created strictly mortal. A future state of immortality is a *possibility* for a person, but that immortality has some conditions tied to it. You've got to live right if you're going to get it. The "good guys" make it to immortality and end up in heaven. The "bad guys" don't. But they don't go to hell; they simply die and are no more. It all depends on what you've done in this mortal life. Fulfill the requirements of proper Christian living and you will be immortal, saved for eternity. Fail to meet those requirements and in the end it will be as if you never existed—just as one more mosquito coming and going unnoticed in a murky Mississippi swamp.

The close cousin, annihilation, is very similar to conditionalism in content. With tongue in cheek, this ideology agrees that there is eternal punishment for the wicked. But there's a catch. The eternal punishment meted out to the evil is the total annihilation of the existence of the wicked for all eternity. Everything about the wicked ceases at death; every ounce of consciousness is gone forever. Not being conscious of anything, that is, simply ceasing to be, is the worst conceivable penalty one could ever suffer—so say the annihilationists.

The major problem for the annihilationists has been trying to explain how extinction can be a punishment to those whose consciousness is extinct. How do you know you're being punished when there is no you to experience the punishment? The idea makes about as much sense as exhuming the body of a dead murderer and hanging it just to teach him a lesson he'll never forget.

It is not surprising that neither of these hitchhikers on the wagon of universalism has made a great impact. There are few adherents of either of them today. In the late eighteenth century, however, they did play some part in softening the hard fact of eternal punishment in the minds of many. In that respect they have a small part in the loss of hell in our time.

Universalism, as powerful as it has been in contributing to the "disappearance" of hell, is devoid of truth. It's dead wrong, and it's a dead-end street. Rejection of the notion is imperative. In the final analysis, it's nothing more than the dream of rebellious creatures seeking to extend their imagined independence from their creator into eternity.

Tennyson, who himself was captivated by the spirit of universalism, summed up the position and its inherent weaknesses well in his *In Memoriam* (under its now well-known caption, "The Larger Hope"):

> The wish, that of the living whole
> No life may fail beyond the grave,
> Derives it not from what we have
> The likest God within the soul?
>
> I stretch lame hands of faith, and grope,
> And gather dust and chaff, and call
> To what I feel is Lord of all,
> And faintly trust the larger hope.[4]

---

[4]*The Complete Poetical Works of Tennyson*, Cambridge edition (Boston: Houghton-Mifflin, 1963), p. 163.

5
Higher Criticism—and Other "Games Scholars Play" _____

Before the nineteenth century, universalism, though not without influence, had difficulty establishing a solid foothold in the church. Those who espoused it were constantly and rightly resisted. Appealing as it was to many, it was so obviously incompatible with the Bible in general and the sayings of Jesus in particular that it never became a best-seller in the religious marketplace. It's proponents simply did not overcome the barrier of the Bible.

The nineteenth century, however, witnessed the beginning of a serious effort to surmount these biblical "problems." F. D. Maurice, one of the more popular and able proponents of universalism in nineteenth-century England, saw the problem clearly, particularly the thorny issue of the words of Jesus about hell. His answer was:

> We feel the necessity of giving up the passages, of supposing that they were not by Him to whom they are attributed, or that He was mistaken. But you dare not take that course.[1]

How revealing, to say the least, because Maurice did take that course! His underlying philosophical presuppositions about the love of God and the will of man pushed him ultimately toward universalism. But he knew the words of Jesus in the Bible didn't back up his position. His answer? Throw out those strong sayings of Jesus regarding eternal punishment. On what grounds? By

---

[1]*Theological Essays,* 3rd edition (London: Macmillan, 1871), p. 444.

suggesting that (1) they were falsely attributed to Jesus or (2) that Jesus was mistaken.

There was no way either of these methods of dealing with Jesus' severe sayings would be accepted in the nineteenth-century English church. Maurice, who later lost his chair at Kings College because of his universalist tendencies, knew it. Hence the last sentence in the quote, "But you dare not take that course." He was correct: One did not dare to hold such a view and expect to be accepted in most quarters of Christendom. He prophesied his own expulsion.

It took the ascendency of modern biblical criticism, the third of the four sources of attack against the truth of hell, to provide an acceptable basis for many who wished the justification to dismiss those "harsh" words the New Testament ascribes to Jesus.

The biblical criticism I refer to here is the destructive higher biblical study which passes judgment on the authority of Scripture. It assumes the responsibility of determining "scientifically" the *actual* sources and the reliability of our Bible.

It should be understood that biblical criticism that accepts the authority of Scripture does have a legitimacy. But if presuppositions for determining reliability are unreliable, it doesn't prove a thing; and so far, even the critics themselves can't agree on how reliable their methods are! Worse than that, as the history of modern biblical higher criticism has unfolded, what has appeared is a ceaseless series of thinly veiled attempts (1) to discredit either much of the Bible's text or (2) to "prove" that the various books of the Bible originated from a complex mixture of sources, each with its own bias to disqualify it. If these two notions are established, interpretations and applications of the Bible, other than those orthodoxy has established, are easily made.

Games "Scholars" Play

There are about as many schemes aimed at questioning the authenticity of the Bible as there are critics who ply this dubious trade. One of the preeminent pioneers of this negative type of biblical criticism was Julius Wellhausen (1844–1910). He decided that the books of the Old Testament had evolved over many centuries from bits and pieces put together, first by one writer, then another, until they at last took their present shape. Another early critic, D. F. Strauss, a contemporary of Wellhausen, arbitrarily tossed out as unauthentic everything supernatural and messianic from the Gospels simply because he had decided the idea of a Messiah and things supernatural couldn't possibly be true. Starting with presuppositions impossible to prove, biblical critics such as these proceed to reinterpret the whole Bible in the light of their unfounded point of beginning.

A steady procession of critics followed the pattern set by these precedent setters, some better and some worse, but *none* good. All worked hard at cutting away at the foundations of the church's historic view of the Bible and its trustworthiness.

The "science" of biblical higher criticism has flowered in the twentieth century in the person of Rudolf Bultmann, perhaps with him more than with anyone else. Here was another man with a bits-and-pieces theory concerning the origin of the books of the Bible. His unique twist was that the bits and pieces were clumps of material originally in oral form only. Slowly, the oral materials were gathered and put in written form. But by the time they got into written form and in the Bible, they were historically inaccurate, in fact not even intended to be accurate! He decided, for example, that the Gospels, Matthew, Mark, Luke, and John, were mostly myths made up by various people and special interest groups in the very ancient church. Few of the statements credited to Jesus actually fell from His lips. People put their own opinions in Jesus' mouth, as it were, in order to give them added weight.

Now it is obviously true that the gospel was in oral form many years before it was written. The Scriptures themselves testify to that. But this in no way presupposes that the divinely inspired Scriptures are inaccurate and actually misrepresent the truth.

Can you guess a set of sayings of Jesus that in particular

Bultmann assures us are not possibly from Him? That's right! Those sayings that deal with eternal torment. Those harsh ideas were the invention of some vindictive folks in the early church who managed to get their material inserted into the text.

Games! These critics play academic, ivy-towered games. As you study the history of biblical criticism you're not sure whether to laugh or cry. You want to laugh because of the myriad of contradictory theories advanced, one on top of the other. You want to cry because of the damage done to so many who accept the "findings" of these scholarly sounding games and, as a result, come to doubt the truth of God.

Higher Criticism: Vitamin for an Ailing Philosophy

Biblical higher criticism was just what the doctor ordered for a seriously-ill universalism. Now those harsh sayings of Jesus about hell could conveniently be brushed under some scholastic rug. It was love at first sight between the universalists and the critics. Almost immediately, there were many marriages of the two philosophies. Not all higher critics buy universalism, but nowadays, the converse is almost always true: Virtually all universalists buy higher criticism.

They *need* each other. The universalists need the higher critics to tidily undermine the authority of the Bible's obvious teaching about hell. The higher critics need the universalists to get them out of hell for tampering with the authority of the Scriptures in general and the words of Jesus Christ in particular.

Yet even the higher critics have had to admit that the Bible *as it actually reads,* authentic or not, teaches the eternal punishment of the wicked. Bultmann concedes that as Jesus is presented in the New Testament, "He expects the resurrection of the dead (Mark 12:18–27) and the judgment (Luke 11:31 ff). He shares the idea of a fiery hell into which the damned are to be cast (Mark 9:43–48; Matthew 10:28)."[2]

---

[2]*Theology of the New Testament,* vol. 1 (New York: Scribner, 1951–55), p. 11.

In a similar vein, another of the critics, T. W. Manson, writing on Luke 12:5 and Matthew 10:28 acknowledges, "In this passage Gehenna [hell] means the place of torment for those who are condemned in the final judgment."[3]

Today, few (if any), even among the most radical critics, question whether the Bible teaches eternal punishment. Rather, they maintain that those sayings in the Bible pack no authority, and their authenticity must be rejected because of the manner in which they made their way into the Bible. Bishop J.A.T. Robinson avoids the plain teaching of the Bible and the orthodox church when he says,

> To express convictions going beyond sight and touch, the Bible, like all ancient literature, projects pictures (not, of course, intended to be taken literally) of "another world" to which people "go" when they die. Subsequent Christian tradition has elaborated these—and often distorted them.[4]

With this statement, the presumptuous bishop writes off nineteen hundred years of interpretation by the church and replaces it with his own. But this effort is not his alone. Many have chosen a similar course.

The New Universalism

Modern biblical higher criticism, gifted at inventing devices for dismissing as unauthentic whatever passages of Scripture it chooses, has proven to be an inestimable boon to universalism. It has been such a boon that in this century we are now confronted with a new brand of universalism—*new universalism*. The new universalists pretend they're different from the old, classical universalists, but this is a smoke screen. The name may be a hair breadth different and the package may have a slightly new look, but the product is the same old thing.

The supposed difference between the "old" and "new" uni-

---

[3]*Sayings of Jesus* (London: SCM Press, 1957), p. 107.
[4]Robinson, *But That I Can't Believe,* pp. 67–68.

versalism is that while old universalism admittedly rested on philosophical assumptions, the new universalism is founded upon "biblical teaching," reinterpreted, of course, in the light of modern criticism. New universalism, we are given to believe, is universalism turned respectable.

Don't you believe it! It's the same old story—the same old universalism based on the same false philosophical foundation. Since universalists couldn't make their doctrine fit the Bible, they finally figured a way to bend the Bible to fit their doctrine.

A classic example of the new universalism is found in a sermon by one of its most able evangelists, Karl Barth. Few men in this century have had the theological influence of this outspoken Continental theologian. In an Easter Sunday sermon delivered at a prison in Basel, Switzerland, Barth assured the inmates,

> God is a very distinguished gentleman whose privilege and enjoyment it is to give freely and to be merciful. Hence he grants eternal life. . . . But now remember also, dear brothers and sisters, that God so acted in Jesus Christ in order that we, truly all of us, without exception, may share in this free gift of eternal life. . . . There [in the Easter story] all of us, mankind itself, were made free for eternal life. . . . Granted all this, what remains there for us to be done? Only one thing: to perceive, to accept, and to take to heart that this is so.[5]

Barth comes so close to the truth, yet he is an eternity away. Convinced that the triumph of God's grace over sin was the overriding principle in the New Testament, Barth made that viewpoint the prism through which the whole New Testament was to be seen and reinterpreted. By this he believed that grace has triumphed for all men, all are saved (even though they don't all know it and may or may not want it.) The only task left is to let everyone know about it!

Such a teaching demanded that the biblical passages offering so obviously a contrary message be forced to undergo a reinterpre-

[5]*Deliverance to the Captives* (New York: Harper & Row, 1961), pp. 148–49.

tation. Any and all contrary sayings from the Bible had to be explained away critically in the light of this one all-consuming fact of "grace."

A more moderate biblical critic stressed the unacceptable nature of universalism well when he wrote:

> Despite its attractiveness, Universalism has many inherent weaknesses that make its untenability as a Christian doctrine extremely dubious and, as the teaching of Jesus, impossible.[6]

Destructive biblical higher criticism isn't a doctrine or a theology. It's a tool to fool—a tool made available by the critic to the public to chisel away from the Bible whatever is not acceptable nor wanted. Out with the chips goes the orthodox doctrine.

In this case, hell is to be chiseled off. The higher critic pretends to honor Jesus but brings the statements ascribed to Him into question. Today's Christians are told that their ancestors in the first two Christian centuries added all that nasty stuff about the place where the worm does not die and the lake of fire is never quenched.

You are free to come up with any doctrinal creation your heart desires, and you can label it with any name that will help it sell. But whatever name is given, there is one that will never fit: Christianity.

I imagine the higher critics have some kind of right to call their game by any name. They can even call it Christianity. But a name can't change what it is or make it what it isn't. With no eternal punishment of the reprobate, we're talking about some off-beat religion seeking to imitate Christianity at certain points as, for example, the Jehovah's Witnesses do. But universalism is not Christianity, and it has no place in the Christian faith.

Universalism then, particularly since it now has the support of modern higher criticism of the Scriptures, has become the single

---

[6]J. Arthur Baird, *The Justice of God in the Teaching of Jesus* (Philadelphia: Westminster Press, 1963), p. 230.

greatest cause for the loss of hell in our time. It has lulled many to sleep with hopes of waking in a dreamland where rebellion and sin against the almighty God of heaven are little noticed or altogether ignored.

But as far as God is concerned, nothing has changed. The forever punishment of the wicked is still as much a part of the outworking of His purposes as it was when He laid the foundation of the earth.

6
Public Education and Spiritual Accountability (Or, Busing May Be the Least of Your Worries!)

Ostensibly far removed from religious matters, American public education has been anything but neutral regarding hell and eternal punishment. Cloaked under the idyllic myth of separation of church and state, public education, with its serious anti-hell and anti-punishment propaganda, is increasingly becoming a front runner in the causes for the decline of the awareness of hell.

Rationalism: The Prevailing Philosophy of Public Education

Educational systems do not exist in a philosophical vacuum, and our American program of public education is no exception. Sitting squarely on a foundation of philosophical rationalism, it perpetuates a philosophical framework committed to calling all phenomena, ideologies, theories, and doctrines confronted by man's experience to be accountable to human reason.

Moral and spiritual matters are by no means exempt from accountability in reason's courtroom. Quite to the contrary, for it is in those areas in particular that reason deems itself more competent to judge.

One of the great voices for the propagation of liberal ideas in the nineteenth century was that of John Stuart Mill. For example, an entry concerning him in an encyclopedia lists this information:

Mill's writings developed existing ideas rather than advanced new ones, but probably they did more than those of anyone else to mold liberal opinion in his time.[1]

The popular nineteenth-century rationalist did not shrink from judging even God Himself.

For it is impossible that any one who habitually thinks, and who is unable to blunt his inquiring intellect by sophistry, should be able without misgiving to go on ascribing absolute perfection to the author and ruler of a so clumsily made and capriciously governed creation as this planet and the life of its inhabitants.[2]

Such a statement gives a clue to the incredibly confident presumption of the rationalist. It is simply postulated that properly equipped, human reason is thoroughly capable of rendering true judgments on all moral and spiritual matters.

Human reason in itself is not an evil thing. However, it is a perversion of reason to exalt it as *the* criterion by which all knowledge and experiences are to be judged. Divorced from the enlightenment of the Holy Spirit, it then becomes a tool for great evil.

The necessary consequence of this perverted use of human reason is a society that steadily, blindly plunges itself deeper and deeper into moral and spiritual darkness. Claiming great wisdom, it becomes exceedingly foolish. God and His revelation of Himself are jettisoned as the standard of truth. Moral relativism is substituted for absolute righteousness. Spiritual darkness parades itself disguised as "enlightened religion." Ignorantly imagining it has displaced the "barbaric" idea of a God who would punish the wicked with the civilized idea of an indulgent, all-tolerant, all-embracing, distant deity who rubber-stamps all of reason's judgments, rationalism hurries off toward hell at an

---

[1] Collier's Encyclopedia, vol. 13 (New York: P. F. Collier and Son, Inc., 1956), p. 603.
[2] John Stuart Mill, *Three Essays,* 3rd edition (London: Longmans, 1874), p. 112.

ever-accelerating pace. And it's all perpetuated in our public schools.

Who can doubt that our public education system is geared to aid and abet this rationalistic mode of operation to which our society is so committed? Though children are generally not told explicitly that God, His Scriptures, and His church are not to be looked to or trusted as determinative for truth and direction in life, the whole thrust of the educational process heads them in the opposite direction. Almost from the first day in school they are led to believe that the goal of their education is to be equipped with the necessary tools so that they will be able to determine truth and right with their own reason. By precept and example they are constantly urged on in that direction.

In this framework God *must* be considered irrelevant because He is completely removed from the educational process. How could a child or a young person possibly come to see the God of heaven as the source of truth or as the One to whom all mankind is accountable when it is against the law to speak positively of Him or talk to Him in the public school classroom? This insidious philosophical rationalism is the only option with which the student is left.

While sitting in an airplane recently, I heard two young women discussing the place the church should fill in a person's life. "I think the church is fine just as long as it doesn't affect the life-styles of the people in it," said one. "It must never be allowed to be a dominant force in our lives," agreed the other.

I could hardly believe my ears! Here were two young ladies who openly admitted that they were limping emotionally because they had just experienced a break-up with the men they had been living with outside of marriage. But nonetheless, they considered their own human reason qualified and competent to judge what role the church of God could properly play in people's lives. The thought never crossed their minds that God might have a determinative role in deciding such matters.

Where did they learn such presumption? Could seventeen years of public education have been a contributing factor? In my opinion, the seeds of this devastating replacement of accountability to God with accountability to one's own educated reason are sown in kindergarten, cultivated in elementary and high school, and harvested in college. Recent years have yielded a bumper crop of students who confidently sit in judgment of God, the Scriptures, and the church. All sense of spiritual accountability to God has been lost.

Hell and Rationalism

The rationalism poured into the students' minds cannot help but make hamburger out of hell. Fallen human reason will not and cannot understand or accept hell. Indeed, if it accepts that there is a hell, human reason must abdicate its exalted position. It must repent and recognize God as *the* final authority in all things. This is the very thing rationalism is not about to do.

Quoting Mill again, we can see clearly the direction that rationalism will inevitably take hell.

> I say nothing of the moral difficulties and perversions involved in revelation itself; though even in the Christianity of the Gospels, at least in its ordinary interpretation, there are some of so flagrant a character as almost to outweigh all the beauty and benignity and moral greatness which so eminently distinguish the sayings and character of Christ. The recognition, for example, of the highest object of worship, in a being who could make a Hell; and who could create countless generations of human beings with the certain foreknowledge that he was creating them for this fate. Is there any moral enormity which might not be justified by imitation of such a Deity?[3]

Rationalism necessarily rejects hell. Few, if any, truths of God offend unregenerate human reason more. Yet the hard facts indicate clearly that God-rejecting, hell- and heaven-denying ra-

---

[3]Ibid., pp. 113–14.

tionalism, bursting in through the doors of secular public education, has gained a pervasive dominance in our society and thus
become an incredibly powerful factor in hell's demise.

Evolution, Death, the Soul, and Hell

A man becomes incurably ill with terminal cancer. His family
and friends are fully aware of the situation. Seldom is the impending death mentioned in the presence of the one dying. As the signs
of the approaching death intensify and the end draws near, the
victim is quietly whisked away to a hospital or rest home where
only a few are spectators to the death drama.

Immediately after death, every effort is made to give the body
the appearance of some serene "normal" tranquility, so that the
family and friends who view the deceased will be bothered mini-
mally with the reality of death. The whole production is skillfully
thought out. It's all a part of our twentieth-century handling of
death.

For most of this century every effort was made to remove death
as far as possible from human experience. Even now the great
majority still seem convinced that if we don't talk about death or
think about death, if we keep it out of sight as much as possible, it
will go away and won't require any further consideration.

Interestingly, there is a significant recent trend to portray the
actual experience of dying as very pleasant. Spearheaded by
writers such as Elisabeth Kubler-Ross and Raymond Moody,[4]
movement toward a much less threatening view of death is definitely under way. Whether or not a more realistic and healthy
attitude will result from such work remains to be seen.

Accounts of serenity and euphoria related by people recently
returned from death's entryway may indeed assuage the haunting
fears many have of the death experience. But these pleasant

---

[4]Elisabeth Kubler-Ross, *On Death and Dying* (New York: Macmillan, 1969);
Raymond Moody, *Life After Life* (New York: Bantam, 1976).

accounts can do nothing to assure the *soul* of what will happen beyond the immediate circumstances of passing from this life.

Further, the reports by Dr. Maurice Rawlings in his recent book, *Beyond Death's Door*,[5] supply ample reason to be suspicious of the new "happy times" theories of dying. Rawlings cautions,

> I am convinced that all of the cases published by Dr. Raymond Moody and Dr. Kubler-Ross, and subsequently by Dr. Karlis Osis and Erlendur Haraldsson in their excellent collection *At The Hour of Death*, [n. Drs. Karlis Osis and Erlendur Haraldsson, *At the Hour of Death* (New York: Avon Books, 1977)] are completely accurately reported by the authors but not always completely recalled or reported by the patients. I have found that most of the bad experiences are soon suppressed deeply into the patient's subliminal or subconscious mind. . . . After many interrogations of patients I have personally resuscitated, I was amazed by the discovery that many have had bad experiences.[6]

Death, for the great majority of people, is still a frightening issue, and the long-range reality of it remains shrouded in deep mystery. Part of the fear surrounding death no doubt involves not knowing what to expect or what physical suffering may accompany death. Infinitely more instrumental and legitimate in producing anxiety about death is the dreaded uneasiness concerning what happens after the death experience. Is there anything there at all? Is my soul immortal? What if it is? How will my conduct in this present life affect the next life—if there is one? What will be my lot?

Until the last century or so, those questions had a fairly common set of answers for people touched by Christendom. Few questioned life after death. The human soul was believed to be immortal, and the next life's direction was cast in this life. But we are part of a brave new era in which those hitherto sure answers

---

[5]*Beyond Death's Door* (Nashville: Thomas Nelson, 1978).
[6]Ibid., pp. 65–66.

are catgorically rejected, blunted, or at least cast in the shadows of doubt. Rejecting positive truth, late twentieth-century man faces the gates of death with uncertainty or with a new bright hopefulness.

So what produced the change in the attitude toward death and immortality? At the root of the answer is a whole new theory as to the origin of man—evolution. Remember, Charles Darwin published his *Origin of Species* in 1859, introducing the popular theory of naturalistic evolution. For those who accepted Darwin's ideas, the door was opened wide to an entirely revamped view of the nature and destiny of man. Answer me: Have or have not the classrooms of America served as the pulpits from which evolution has been preached?

As it was commonly developed, the theory of naturalistic evolution cut away at critical areas of orthodox Christian doctrine. Moral accountability and the immortality of the soul went up for grabs and were usually lost somewhere in thin air simply because they fit nowhere. Accountability to whom? Some primordial amoeba? Immortality of what soul? The net effect of the loss of truth in those two areas alone was almost terminal for the doctrine of eternal punishment. Without moral accountability, there is no basis for judgment; there isn't even a judge. Without immortality, there can be no life after death for which to hold the slightest concern.

Yet the theory of naturalistic evolution has not been able to contribute any certain knowledge about the mysteries of existence beyond the grave. A humanity that was once sure of the options regarding life after death is no longer sure of anything. It's not sure there's something; it's not sure there's nothing. If there is something, it's not sure it's good; it's not sure it's bad. Agnosticism now reigns for creatures who apparently haven't evolved enough yet to live in confidence without knowing what comes with death.

Modern man's story is this: Like a kitten in a sandbox, cover

65

the unwanted as best you can. Make light of the loose ends you can't tuck into some neat pigeon hole. Joke about death. Be as convincing as possible that everything is going to turn out all right. Adopt the Mother Goose philosophy that everyone is going to live happily ever after.

Is that not precisely where modern education has gone with death, immortality, judgment, and hell? Ask some questions of those who have adopted the evolutionary hypothesis. Few are bold enough to categorically deny any possibility of immortality, judgment, heaven, and hell. What you will generally find is a murky cloud of uneasiness about these items. At the same time, unconvincing theories multiply as to how they may be properly disposed of. Natural selection may have evolved a mortal soul, but it has been unable to successfully persuade its creation there is no forever hell.

Rejecting the biblical and orthodox doctrine of the creation of man, the theory of naturalistic evolution (and theory is all it is!) is by necessity forced to accept man as the present plateau in a dragging-on-forever process of development, hopefully from lower to higher life. This man has no discernible purpose, and he moves toward no terminal goal. Locked into a process he cannot speed up, slow down, or get out of, he exists. That's it. That's *all* of it; he just exists.

But he won't go to hell when he dies. He hopes he won't go anywhere, because there's (hopefully) nowhere to go. Having developed from some infinitely low form, whatever soul he may have cannot possess meaning and significance. The life and death of any one individual of the species is nothing more nor less than one more meaningless moment in an endless, purposeless, goalless, hopeless chain of existences. Hell, heaven, and judgment are concepts not even viable for discussion with such a being.

Pathetic as the fruit of the theory of evolution is, its devotees prefer to remain ignorant on the subject of immortality. To come up for air would mean facing the reality of human experience for a change. The hard facts of the reality of a soul created by God and having a destiny would have to be faced. Above all, the stark reality of hell, of eternal punishment for rebellion against God Almighty, would have to be looked directly in the face.

One suspects that the evolutionary hypotheses are so popular because, if man's origin in God can be set aside, so can his destiny. Thus, in the final analysis, evolution is one more futile attempt to do away with hell.

I cannot help but speculate that Darwin was in some measure himself motivated to his conclusions in the *Origin of Species* by his own personal rejection of hell. Here are his own shockingly revealing words on the subject:

> . . . disbelief crept over me at a very slow rate, but was at last complete. . . . I can hardly see how anyone ought to wish Christianity to be true; for, if so, the plain language of the text seems to show that the men who do not believe—and this would include my father, brother, and almost all my best friends—will be everlastingly punished. And this is a damnable doctrine.[7]

Quite an unscientific reaction from one who was supposedly a man of science! And isn't it amazing that those who preach a literal hell are so often accused of emotionalism? This reaction of Darwin's against hell is emotionalism at its height! I get the distinct impression that those who reject the reality of hell stoop to far more emotionalism than any of the so-called preachers of doom. Indeed, on what other grounds than emotionalism could the rejector of future punishment rest his case? He has no factual, observable, scientific data at his disposal.

Yes, God-denying naturalistic evolution has taken a great toll in the loss of hell. The confusion, obscurity, and agnosticism it has wrapped about man on matters concerning his precious soul's destiny have heavily contributed to hell's demise—simply by

---

[7]Quoted in Leslie Weatherhead, *The Christian Agnostic* (London: Hodder and Stoughton, 1965), p. 164.

placing the whole matter beyond the realm of certainty. It has taken the edge off eternity for altogether too many, and it is this "doctrine" that is taught in many public school classrooms. Public education, with evolution as a key dogma, has contributed massively to the decline of hell, and it has done nothing to replace the resultant void in moral accountability.

7
The High Middle Ages and Hell_____

Many a bitter critic of the orthodox doctrine of hell persists in the argument that the church's hard line on eternal punishment is nothing more than a medieval hangover. Insisting that Jesus (and the Bible) never intended to mean that hell was a place of forever torment, the critics shrug off such a doctrine as nothing more than a lingering blackness invented in the Dark Ages.

This is an intriguing thesis, but is it true? Learning the answer to this question demands some knowledge of the doctrine of hell as it was understood in the Middle Ages. So in this chapter we'll first examine briefly the popular portrayal of hell in medieval times. Then, secondly, we'll look at the theological understanding of hell in that era as expressed by several medieval theologians. Then we will be able to conclude whether or not the church of the Middle Ages warped the biblical view of hell and thereby produced a distortion that still shadows the truth in much of the modern church.

Popular Thought on Hell in the Middle Ages

Theological treatment of religious subjects was extremely complex and varied in the Middle Ages. The scholastics of that period have left an indelible mark on the history of theology with their intricate disputations on such subjects as, "How many angels can dance on the point of a needle?"

Such highly involved thought was not, however, characteristic of the common people of that historical period. In almost every age there has been some difference in level of thought between the man on the street and the technical theologian. The Middle Ages were no exception.

Specifically, in the Middle Ages there was a fairly definable conception of the doctrine of eternal punishment held by the common people. The classic description of that understanding is found in the work of Dante, the brilliant Florentine poet.

Though not devoid of theological understanding, Dante was not a theologian, and his work must not be viewed as the standard-bearer of a theological treatise of the medieval western church. But the *Divine Comedy,* his epic poem, dramatically captured the prevailing popular thought of many a medieval man about hell. This literary masterpiece became the standard for the thought, content, and style concerning the subject for popular western writers in subsequent centuries.

In one section of another of his poems, *The Inferno,* Dante described himself being led by the Roman poet, Virgil, on a journey through the awesome sights of hell. Imagining hell to be a cone-shaped pit of nine levels of progressively worse torment, Dante observed the damned of the ages writhing in great agony for their misdeeds. At one point his eye caught a pit of boiling lava. He described tormented souls in the pit jumping above the lava to free themselves of the searing heat, if but for a brief moment:

> All my attention was fixed upon the pitch:
> to observe the people who were boiling in it,
> and the customs and the punishments of that ditch.
>
> As dolphins surface and begin to flip
> their arched backs from the sea, warning the sailors
> to fall-to and begin to secure ship—
>
> So now and then, some soul, to ease his pain,
> showed us a glimpse of his back above the pitch
> and quick as lightning disappeared again.[1]

[1]Dante, *The Inferno,* p. 191.

A bit farther on he observed:

One lay gasping on another's shoulder,
   one on another's belly; and some were crawling
   on hands and knees among the broken boulders.

Silent, slow step by step, we moved ahead
   looking at and listening to those souls
   too weak to raise themselves from their stone bed.

I saw two there like two pans that are put
   one against the other to hold their warmth.
   They were covered with great scabs from head to foot.

No stable boy in a hurry to go home,
   or for whom his master waits impatiently,
   ever scrubbed harder with his currycomb

than those two spirits of the stinking ditch
   scrubbed at themselves with their own bloody claws
   to ease the furious burning of the itch.

And as they scrubbed and clawed themselves, their nails
   drew down the scabs the way a knife scrapes bream
   or some other fish with even larger scales.[2]

This kind of description helped establish a framework for a popular understanding of hell for many centuries. Personally, I believe Dante's insight is brilliantly magnificent. Dante was well aware that his description of hell's torments was speculative and imaginative. Frankly, the problem with his work as it relates to contemporary doubts concerning hell is not that he produced a speculative treatment of hell, but that many subsequent readers, imitative writers, and preachers *forgot these descriptions were speculations and treated them rather as theological dogma.* Thus, Dante's speculations sometimes metamorphosed into dogmatic theological formulations in the minds of many common people. Fiction turned to fact does not and cannot breed healthy

---

[2]Ibid., p. 245.

doctrine. Dante's work when misapplied, which it often has been, has become somewhat of a contributing factor to hell's going out of style.

Admittedly, the popular view of hell that evolved in the Middle Ages too often included incredibly far-fetched, speculative trappings. It is these speculative excesses that have opened medieval people to so much criticism on this subject in later centuries. But we must not forget that writings such as Dante's were never intended to be standards of orthodoxy, and those who identify them as such are either unfair or don't have a clear notion of what orthodoxy really is.

Let me say again that the basic "medieval problem" is not Dante and others like him; the problem is the critics who unfairly use him for theological target practice. Suppose that three hundred years from now someone were to ask what people believed about the devil and temptation in the twentieth century. A copy of C. S. Lewis's book, *The Screwtape Letters,* is found in a musty file. After exhaustive reading, a group of twenty-third century scholars conclude that people in Lewis's day most certainly conversed regularly with a little demon named Wormwood. Can't you see what happens? *Screwtape Letters* is a useful book, but it is not a technical theological treatise. Neither Dante nor Lewis wrote intending to form foundational doctrine. Though certainly the methods of both have a place in expressing Christian thought, they were not formal theological writers in their respective times.

That Dante's influence was felt far beyond the Middle Ages is dramatically witnessed in another literary high-water mark—the writings of the English poet, Milton. Although writing three and a half centuries later, in many ways Milton styled himself after Dante. In *Paradise Lost,* Milton graphically described the fall of Satan and his angels from heaven. Immediately after his arrival in hell, Satan looked around at the misery and destruction there. This is what Milton wrote that the eye of Satan saw:

At once, as far as Angels ken [understand, grasp],
he views
The dismal situation waste and wild:
A dungeon horrible on all sides round
As one great furnace flamed; yet from those flames
No light; but rather darkness visible
Served only to discover sights of woe,
Regions of sorrow, doleful shades, where peace
And rest can never dwell, hope never comes
That comes to all; but torture without end
Still urges, and a fiery deluge, fed
With ever-burning sulphur unconsumed,
Such place Eternal Justice had prepared
For those rebellious; here their prison ordained
In utter darkness, and their portion set,
As far removed from God and light of Heaven
As from the centre thrice to the utmost pole.
Oh, how unlike the place from whence they fell![3]

Too many contemporaries read Milton as a great literary genius whose content was mad and a holdover from the Dark Ages. Literary genius he was; madman he was not. He was undoubtedly influenced by Dante, and like his predecessor, Milton's description of hell was speculative. *Paradise Lost* is patently not a textbook of systematic theology, nor was it ever so intended. It is thoroughly legitimate literature. Milton's account of hell is not to be viewed as Scripture inspired by the Holy Spirit; it is fictional. Unfortunately, as with Dante, Milton's legacy to the future was negative in regard to hell's staying in style. But Milton certainly cannot be held accountable for such a result. It was others, not he, who erred by misapplying his work.

What we actually have, in effect, from Dante and a host of other popular writers and preachers of the Middle Ages, is a synthesis of popular medieval thought that reached out far beyond that period. It need not be denied that some literary artisans

---

[3]Milton, *Paradise Lost,* book I, p. 79.

of that era supplied speculative content to the doctrine of eternal punishment that is not found in Scripture or the primitive church. Attempts to dogmatize these popular, speculative accounts have worked against maintaining a wholesome, proper, and balanced perspective on hell in our own time. But should these medieval writers be accused of being the *cause* for hell's demise in the twentieth century? Absolutely not! It's unfortunate that some of the medieval age's fear of hell is not part of our own generation.

Theological Thought on Hell in the Middle Ages

To judge the formal theology of the medieval church by the literary works of Dante and others less gifted than he is simply not fair play. Who, in the name of fairness, would make the well-known book *The Robe* (by Lloyd C. Douglas) the theological standard of Christology for the twentieth-century church? The theology of our time must be judged by the work of its theologians and not by every popular writer who takes pen in hand. And, in the same way, the theology of the medieval church must not be judged without considering the work of its theologians.

It is neither possible nor necessary to present an exhaustive study of medieval theology here. I know of no historian of theology who questions whether the theologians of the Middle Ages maintained the view of a real place of punishment that was to last forever. I include a sampling of the work of the medieval era's theologians only to make it plainly evident that the doctrine of eternal retribution for the wicked has consistent continuity throughout the history of the church—from the day of Pentecost until this present hour.

First, let's dispel a false notion about the era we are about to consider: These are not the "Dark Ages," at least not theologically. It is true that during part of the period from the collapse of the Roman Empire in the West until the end of the fifteenth century, there were significant barbarian invasions and the general social, political, economic, and religious climate of Europe was not always the best. Yet, though fine theological scholarship was not as evident as before and after the Middle Ages, some theological work was absolutely exceptional.

This is noted because so many modern readers have been led to believe that all medievals were ignorant illiterates. Nothing could be further from the truth. It is readily granted that the Scholastic doctors were often caught up in infinitely technical philosophical and theological speculation. But ignorant and illiterate they were not.

The representative theologians we will consider here were not backwoods barbarians. Agobard (769-840) was the forty-fourth bishop of Lyons. Incredibly productive, he was a bold leader of the ninth-century church. Anselm of Canterbury (1033-1109) is perhaps even now not fully understood. His *Cur Deus Homo?* (*Why Did God Become Man?*) ranks as one of the most sophisticated theological works ever written.

No survey of medieval theology, regardless of how short it might be, would be representative without including The Theologian, the "Angelic-doctor," Thomas Aquinas (1225-1274). You may disagree with him much, but you dare not disagree that he was one of the outstanding theologians of all history and certainly the greatest medieval theologian. His *Summa Theologicae,* which is a summary of Christian thought as he understood it, is brilliant in its reasoned character. Aquinas must be respected as a great pace-setter in medieval and modern theology.

These three thinkers, Agobard, Anselm, and Aquinas, I have selected as being representative of the medieval church in the West. To their testimony regarding hell I will add that of the Fourth Lateran Council, a council of the Roman church in A.D. 1215. It is this council that the Roman church reckons as the Twelfth Ecumenical Council. Obviously, then, the council's decrees are assuredly representative of the medieval western church.

Punishment as Eternal

Almost without exception medieval theology accepted and perpetuated the orthodox doctrine of hell. Anselm, in a chapter entitled "The Soul Which Despises The Supreme Being Will Be Eternally Wretched," described the fate of the evil:

> So then, nothing can be seen to follow more consistently, and nothing ought to be believed more assuredly, than that man's soul was created in such a way that if it despises loving the Supreme Being it will suffer eternal wretchedness. Consequently, just as the loving soul will rejoice in an eternal reward, so the despising soul will grieve in eternal punishment. And as the former will experience immutable sufficiency, so the latter will experience inconsolable need.[4]

Similar statements could be summoned from scores of other medieval churchmen. The point is that virtually all of them believed in eternal torment for the wicked.

The Wicked Receive the Opposite of the Just

A theme evident in Anselm's statement (above) reoccurs over and over again among theologians of the Middle Ages: Namely, the opposite eternal conditions of the wicked and the righteous. There wasn't a flicker of an idea that the righteous would be rewarded with eternal bliss while the evil would simply fade out of the picture or be ultimately saved. The glorious eternal blessing of the saved is contrasted with the equal and opposite eternal suffering of the evil. In his catechetical instructions, Thomas Aquinas spelled this out:

> It must also be known that the condition of the damned will be the exact contrary to that of the blessed. Theirs is the state of eternal punishment, which has a fourfold evil condition. The bodies of the damned will not be brilliant: "Their countenances shall be as faces burnt" [Isa. 13:8]. Likewise they shall be passible, because they

---

[4]*Monologion* 71, taken from *Anselm of Canterbury,* ed. and trans. Jasper Hopkins and Herbert Richardson (Toronto: The Edwin Mellen Press, 1974), pp. 80-81.

shall never deteriorate and, although burning eternally with fire, they shall never be consumed: "Their worm shall not die and their fire shall not be quenched." They will be weighed down, and the soul of the damned be as it were chained therein: "To bind their kings with fetters, and their nobles with manicles of iron." Finally, they will be in a certain manner fleshly both in soul and body: "The beasts have rotted in their dung."[5]

I'd say that leaves little doubt as to what Aquinas thought about this question! The righteous are eternally blessed and the evil are eternally punished. There is no middle course.

Degrees of Punishment and Reward

In yet another sense Middle Ages theologians were more precise on a point of orthodoxy concerning hell than are many moderns who consider themselves orthodox: degrees of punishment and reward. The Scriptures teach (as I'll show in a later chapter) and the church has steadily held that not all of the evil will receive the same degree of punishment, nor will all of the righteous be rewarded in precisely the same way.

As representative of this understanding, I have chosen to quote Agobard of Lyons. He is not in the same league theologically with Anselm or Aquinas. Yet, as a solid theologian, he well expressed the view of his day. Here is an excerpt from a sermon he preached in 829 or 830.

> Yet one must know that, as "in the Father's house are many rooms" for diversity or worth, so dissimilarity of offense subjects the damned in the fires of Gehenna to different punishments. This Gehenna by no means burns all with one and the same quality, although there is only one Gehenna. These punishments torture beyond strength the ones plunged into it; and even while extinguishing in them the bulwark of life the punishments keep them alive that the end may punish life, seeing that one may live forever without cessation of torment, for one hastens through tortures toward an end, but failing he endures without end. It becomes therefore for

---

[5]*The Catechetical Instruction of St. Thomas Aquinas,* trans. and commentary Rev. Joseph B. Collins (New York: Joseph T. Wagner, 1939), p. 62.

wretched ones a deathless death, an endless end, a ceaseless cessation, since death lives, the end ever begins, and cessation knows not how to cease.[6]

Such a sermon captured the general thought of Abogard's time. Orthodox to the core, it is evident he saw a place of punishment that was eternal, a place in contrast to the blessings of heaven, and where the degree of punishment is directly related to the degree of offense. Without doubt this sermon characterizes the thought of theologians from the fifth to the fifteenth century.

Summarizing the medieval theological understanding of hell, let me refer briefly to the documents of the Fourth Lateran Council. This council, held in 1215, was undoubtedly the most important council of the medieval church. Of judgment, the men of this council confessed,

We firmly believe and affirm also that judgment by Jesus Christ will be individually for those who have lived in this flesh, and that they will receive either punishments or rewards.[7]

And further, of Jesus Christ's coming to judge, they affirmed that He was

. . . to come at the end of time, to judge the living and the dead, and to render to each according to his works, to the wicked as well as to the elect, all of whom will rise with their bodies which they now bear, that they may receive according to their works whether these works have been good or evil, the latter everlasting punishment with the devil, and the former everlasting glory with Christ.[8]

Is this the wildly speculative description of hell that many of us were taught to believe was held by all people in the Dark Ages?

---

[6]*Early Medieval Theology,* trans. and ed. George E. McCracken (Philadelphia: Westminster Press, 1951), p. 354.

[7]Taken from Heinrich J. Denzinger, *The Sources of Catholic Dogma,* trans. Roy J. Deferrari, from the 13th edition of *Enchridion Symbolorum* (St. Louis: B. Herder Co., 1955), p. 168.

[8]Ibid., p. 169.

Quite to the contrary, it is a thoroughly biblical, thoroughly orthodox, and thoroughly sane statement to which orthodox evangelical Christians of all ages could subscribe.

The understanding of the medieval church about hell was orthodox. That's the fact of the matter. Though it must be acknowledged that many writers embellished scriptural accounts with a significant degree of fanciful speculation, nevertheless, our ancestors in the Middle Ages surely bore the torch of orthodoxy with regard to the eternal punishment of the wicked. To accuse them of doing otherwise is to ignore the plain facts of history.

8
The Classical Protestant Preachers

The Jon E. in my name is really a reflection of some high aspirations my parents had for me. They specifically had in mind the great eighteenth-century preacher and theologian, Jonathan Edwards, when they chose my first and middle names.

Jonathan Edwards (in my totally objective opinion!) was one of the truly great thinkers this nation has ever produced. His *Freedom of the Will* (written in 1754) remains a masterpiece. Seldom, however, is he remembered today for his contributions to theology. Rather, it is for a single sermon—"Sinners in the Hands of An Angry God''—that people in our time remember the name of Jonathan Edwards.

No doubt about it, that sermon was dynamite. It epitomizes well much of the preaching on hell within the ranks of classical Protestantism, and it is for that purpose we consider Edwards and that sermon here.

Edwards considered unrepentant man to be hopelessly and desperately wicked. With eloquence and accuracy he described the inner state of the unregenerate:

> The corruption of the heart of man is immoderate and boundless in its fury; and while wicked men live here, it is like fire pent up by God's restraints, whereas if it were let loose, it would set on fire the course of nature; and as the heart is now a sink of sin, so, if sin was not restrained, it would immediately turn the soul into a fiery oven, or a furnace of fire and brimstone.[1]

---

[1]*Edwards' Works,* vol. 6 (New York: Burt Franklin, 1968), p. 453.

Hell's critics point to Edwards and preachers like him with an accusing finger. "All that hell-fire and damnation preaching drove people away from God," they say. Of course the critics' implication is that Edwards and his kind were grossly in error for preaching about hell the way they did. Having lived two hundred years ago, these "naive" preachers can be excused because of ignorance, but with today's enlightenment there is no place for such preaching.

Whether classical Protestant preaching about hell was true or not is to be addressed in this chapter. There is, however, one item that obviously does not require discussion: You won't find classical preaching of this vein coming from today's Protestant ministers.

Ignoring the Reformation emphasis on hell, preachers nowadays seldom speak of it. When they do, it's with a very light step. They aren't about to hurt anyone's feelings by suggesting that some in their congregations may well end up in hell.

The aim of this chapter is to give a sample of classical American Protestantism's understanding of hell and to show that it was correct in its emphasis and content with respect to hell. We will also consider one moderate theological imbalance from the Reformation that did affect much Protestant preaching about hell, one that has contributed somewhat to its loss in our time.

Classical Protestant Preaching

Turning our attention once again to Edwards, notice how imminent he considered the danger of hell to the unrepentant sinner:

> Unconverted men walk over the pit of hell on a rotten covering, and there are innumerable places in this covering so weak that they will not bear their weight, and these places are not seen.[2]

He describes the threat to sinner in terms not at all unlike Dante and Milton:

---

[2]Ibid, pp. 453–54.

Whatever Happened to Hell?

> The wrath of God burns against them, their damnation does not
> slumber; the pit is prepared, the fire is made ready, the furnace is
> now hot, ready to receive them; the flames do now rage and glow.
> The glittering sword is whet, and held over them, and the pit hath
> opened its mouth under them.[3]

While there is more restraint and less speculation here than
there was from the majority of medieval writers and preachers,
the intensity is perhaps even greater. There is a passion here
Dante never knew. Dramatic? There is no question about that!
Personally, I believe it is great preaching. It's certainly a far cry
from those pusillanimous men of present-day cloth who water
down the stark reality of God's truth in the name of propriety.

Hell is a grave reality. People must be made aware of the
danger. Imagine yourself near a three hundred foot cliff on a pitch
dark night. You are about to step over the edge into thin air; in
fact you are only inches away. Standing close by is someone quite
aware the precipice is there. Hearing you pass by he knows the
impending danger to your life.

Now suppose, believing your life and welfare is none of his
business, he says absolutely nothing. That's pitiful, and he's
liable for your life. Or imagine that you are but one second from
stepping over and he says, "Now I would like to call to your
attention that if you proceed on your present course, you will find
there are matters awaiting you that will be found detrimental to
your well-being. . . . Oh, what a pity, there he goes."

When someone is in immediate danger and you know it and can
warn him, you cry out, "Stop!" at the top of your lungs. You
aren't to be blamed if he replies, "Keep your nose out of my
business; I'll take care of my own affaaaaaaiiirrrss. . . ."

Furthermore, you cannot be intimidated if someone else
present, whether aware of the danger or not, says, "Don't be so

---

[3]Ibid, p. 452.

offensive and dramatic; it's not cultured to speak so harshly." You do what you must to save the life and pay no attention to critics.

So it was with our courageous Protestant forebears. They saw the danger and cried out a warning against it. Criticisms from their own contemporaries or moderns were meaningless. There was a responsibility to fulfil, and they met that obligation well.

Edwards was not the only Protestant to preach hell with such fervor. Sermons and writings similar to his are found in the surviving works of many others. The forebodings of hell they signal are more than appropriate. We cannot continue without giving samples of four of the most prominent and worthy men, two American and two English.

Thomas Hooker

The eloquent Cambridge graduate, Thomas Hooker, is one case in point. After being silenced by the tyrannical Archbishop Laud, this powerful Puritan preacher emigrated to America from England in 1633. Three years later he moved with his entire congregation to the banks of the Connecticut River where together they founded the city of Hartford. This was no obscure and ignorant backwoods parson. On the contrary, he was a dynamic leader, active in the early life of this country, especially in the framing of the now famous Connecticut Constitution.

Hooker's preaching fare was not limited to hell. Yet he did not leave hell out of his preaching. A marvelous example of his views on hell, "The Soul's Preparation for Christ; or a Treatise of Contrition," was given in London in 1632.

Conceive thus much, if all the diseases in the world did seize on one man, and if all torments that all the tyrants in the world could devise, were cast upon him; and if all the creatures in heaven and earth did conspire the destruction of this man; and if all the devils in hell did labor to inflict punishments upon him, you would think this man to be in a miserable condition. And yet all this is but a beam of God's indignation. If the beams of God's indignation be so hot, what is the full sum of his wrath, when it shall seize upon the soul of a sinful creature in full measure?[4]

That from one of the founding fathers of Connecticut!

Thomas Shepard

A contemporary of Hooker, Thomas Shepard sailed from England in 1635 and settled first in Boston. Shortly thereafter he took a pastorate in Cambridge, assuming an active role in the founding of nothing less than Harvard University. The following soul-melting dialogue is from his "The Sincere Convert" written in 1641. Speaking of the final judgment, Shepard wrote:

. . . In regard of the fearful sentence that then shall be passed upon thee: "Depart, thou cursed creature, into everlasting fire, prepared for the Devil and his Angels!" Thou shalt then cry out: "O mercy Lord! O a little mercy!" "No," will the Lord Jesus say, "I did indeed once offer it you, but you refused; therefore depart!"

Then thou shalt plead again: "Lord, if I must depart, yet bless me before I go!"

"No, no, Depart, thou cursed!"

"O, but Lord, if I must depart cursed let me go to some good place!"

"No! Depart, thou cursed, into hell fire!"

"O Lord, that's a torment I cannot bear; but if it must be so, Lord, let me come out again quickly!"

"No, Depart, thou cursed, into everlasting fire!"

"O Lord, if this be thy pleasure that here I must abide let me have good company with me!"

"No! Depart, thou cursed, into everlasting fire, prepared for the Devil and his Angels!"

This shall be thy sentence, the hearing of which may make the rocks to rent.[5]

Now that's mighty potent material from one of the founders of what many consider to be our nation's premier university. This

---

[4]William P. Trent and Benjamin W. Wells, eds., *Colonial Prose and Poetry,* "The Transplanting Culture" (New York: Thomas Y. Crowell, 1910), p. 226.
[5]Ibid, pp. 242–43.

was neither unusual nor uncommon preaching in his time. The message was characteristic of the classic early American Protestant pulpiteer.

Isaac Watts

Some time after Hooker and Shepard, the father of English hymns, the "dissenter," Isaac Watts, introduced "man-made hymns" in England. That is, he wrote hymns that weren't taken directly from the Bible. The impact in England and America of the doctrine of Watts's more than six hundred hymns was staggering. They did, and still do, reflect the tenor of classic Protestantism. In an ode, "The Day of Judgment," Watts penned:

> Hopeless mortals! how they scream and shiver while
> devils push them into the pit wide yawning
> Hideous and gloomy to receive them headlong
> Down to the center.[6]

Said Watts in a sermon on the text, "where their worm does not die, and the fire is not quenched" (Mark 9:48):

> It is confessed, that a discourse on this dreadful subject is not a direct ministration of grace and the glad tidings of salvation, yet it has a great and happy tendency to the same end, even the salvation of sinful men; for it awakens them to a more piercing sight, and to a more keen sensation of their own guilt and danger; it possesses their spirits with a more lively sense of misery, it fills them with a holy dread of divine punishment and excites the powerful passion of fear to make them fly from the wrath to come, and betake themselves to the grace of God revealed in the gospel.[7]

Not only Watts, but most classic, mainline Protestant spokesmen understood this kind of explanation as the major apologetic for including the subject of eternal punishment within the bounds of balanced preaching.

---

[6]"The Day of Judgment," stanza VII, *Watts' Works*, vol. 4, 1st edition (New York: AMS Press, 1971), p. 441.

[7] Ibid, vol. 2, p. 267.

Charles Haddon Spurgeon

We need to consider one more Protestant preacher, the marvelously eloquent and persuasive Charles Spurgeon. Audiences at London's six-thousand-seat Metropolitan Tabernacle in the second half of the nineteenth century were enthralled by the sermons of this golden-tongued Baptist. Not lagging behind Dante and Milton in imagination, Spurgeon proclaimed of hell:

> There is a real fire in hell, as truly as you have a real body—a fire exactly like that which we have on this earth, except this: that it will not consume though it will torture you. You have seen asbestos lying amid red hot coals, but not consumed. So your body will be prepared by God in such a way that it will burn forever without being consumed. With your nerves laid raw by searing flame, yet never desensitized for all its raging fury, and the acrid smoke of the sulphurous fumes searing your lungs and choking your breath, you will cry out for the mercy of death, but it shall never, never, no never give you surcease.[8]

Was Preaching on Hell Harmful?

Somehow, through the strange quirks of history, these five well-known Protestant preachers—along with many of their contemporaries—have been assigned the reputation of being "hell-fire and damnation" preachers. It is as though they were evil for warning against hell as they did. Such a judgment on them is as phony as a three-dollar bill. Sure, they preached on hell, among other things. Yes, their preaching was womewhat dramatic. How can one be genuinely honest in preaching hell without a degree of emotion showing through? The gospel is, after all, a somewhat emotional subject!

The truth is these men, and a multitude like them, did not contribute to hell's disappearance as some shallow observers never tire of insisting. Absolutely to the contrary, in their sphere

---

[8]Quoted in Edward Fudge, "Putting Hell In Its Place," *Christianity Today* (6 August 1976), p. 14.

of influence, they were directly responsible for keeping hell in proper focus in the minds and hearts of their hearers. Granted, there were preachers of considerably less ability and balance who tried to imitate them, and a few of them overworked the subject. The temptation to sensationalism and hyper-emotionalism proved too great for a handful.

But even that kind of distortion of the subject is not nearly as disastrous to the truth on hell as is the tragedy of avoiding it or leaving it out altogether. Even worse is the fatal mistake of rejecting hell—using the preaching on hell by men of God as a feeble excuse for rebelling against the whole truth of God. Hell will be filled with rebels against God. Those who fabricate excuses to reject His truth about eternal damnation would do well to take note.

A Theological Imbalance from the Reformation

Newton's third law is that to every action there is an equal and opposite reaction. That principle of physics has a counterpart in theology—at least when imbalances appear. One theological imbalance is likely to produce another at some point—in the opposite direction.

The Protestant Reformation was not immune to theological imbalances in reaction to the Roman church. Not even the most ardent Romanist argues that there were not some serious and dangerous theological imbalances, distortions, and perversions in the Roman church at the dawn of the sixteenth century. Martin Luther was far from being the first and only Roman priest to bemoan the state of doctrinal and moral disarray in the western church of that era. Take, for example, Menot, a sixteenth-century Frenchman who wrote:

> Ho, Lord Jesus, planter of this vine, the Church, behold and visit this vine. Alas! Lord, I think that this year and in the future you will not gather much fruit from your vine, because already it has been dried up for more than fifty years, nor do we have great hope for it

Whatever Happened to Hell?

> unless a fresh planting be made, for there is neither a stalk nor a branch which is of any value.[9]

When Menot was asked why no one corrected abuses if they were so great, he replied that there was no one in the church who had the spirit and zeal to do so.

> Never has the world been so disordered as now, nor in the Church has there been less devotion . . . this is the last hour. . . . I fear that the world will come to an end shortly.[10]

Menot continued his lamentation over the state of the church:

> There was one Judas among the twelve apostles; would that there were one Peter or Andrew among twelve bishops or priests today![11]

Ranking high among problems of the Reformation era was the obscurity, confusion, and outright heresy that had developed over the life and death issue of how justification before God is gained. Call it Pelagianism, semi-Pelagianism, or "works salvation" (they're all the same thing), much of the church supported a doctrine of justification by works. Standing with God was to be gained on the basis of human merit. If for no other reason, the lucrative indulgence trade demanded this means of justification. Who would have paid hard-earned money to buy indulgences if right standing with God (justification) was to be gained by faith, apart from any amount of merit based on personal works—your own or someone else's? No one, of course, and an ill-motivated pope was fully aware of it.

So it was that justification by faith became early the main battle cry of the Reformers against the Roman church. Many Reformers accurately regained the thoroughly orthodox doctrine of justification by faith that had been characteristic of ancients such as

---

[9]E. Jane Dempsey Douglas, *Justification in Late Medieval Preaching* (Leiden: E. J. Brill, 1966), pp. 96–97.
[10]Ibid.
[11]Ibid.

Saint Augustine and Saint John Chrysostom. But in the full, broad spectrum of the Protestant revolution, the emphasis on justification by faith was not always equally healthy either in its content or in the comparative weight given to it with respect to the whole scope of proper Christian doctrine. There were quarters where the reaction was both equal and opposite to the error. If one must choose between errors, perhaps the Reformation's reaction was better than the perversion. Still, it was itself off center in the opposite direction.

That opposite effect tended to boost justification by faith to the number one slot as *the* all-consuming doctrine of Chrstianity, the theme around which all other Christian doctrine must revolve. Good works for any reason were sometimes treated as useless, or even evil. Others ignored sin as irrelevant for the justified. Though these perversions of the biblical orthodox doctrine of justification came in various sizes, shapes, and forms, they were in error nevertheless.

By no means did all Protestants accept these distortions, but too many, in the white heat of battle against heresy, were influenced by them. More than four centuries have not succeeded in completely rectifying that over-reaction in Protestant ranks. In particular modern fundamentalism and broad segments of evangelicalism (both of which we will consider later) have been heavily infected with overkill on justification, though the effect has not been limited to them.

Justification by faith is a true doctrine, but if it is made *the* doctrine of Christianity and exalted above such doctrines as those of the Trinity, the Incarnation and the lordship of the exalted Christ, the road to spiritual and theological health and balance is blocked.

As it relates to hell, the result of theological imbalance on justification has been an insidious, creeping, and personal callousness toward holiness and perseverance. Assure the once-justified that they never again need be concerned with the dire consequences of sinning, no matter how grossly they might in fact sin, and hell becomes a reality—for everyone else. Only the "other guy" can go there. If the justified person believes that hell could never again under any circumstances be any threat to him, he can now lie, cheat, steal, fornicate—maybe even murder—with no fear of eternal retribution.

Permanent, guaranteed immunity to hell, regardless of the offense, causes a hardened indifference in anyone to the reality of God's judgment. Dynamic, *active* faith and trust in Jesus Christ for salvation is then easily replaced by academic assent (often misnamed "faith") to a warped, isolated form of the doctrine of justification. In this manner many who heartily hold a formally orthodox doctrine of hell, hold it with a highly contagious indifference that has contributed to the loss of respect for God in our time.

9
Hell and the Fundamentalist-Evangelical Movements _____

The two current movements most ardent in their support of the doctrine of eternal punishment—and their relationship to its present loss—remain to be surveyed: *fundamentalism* and *evangelicalism*.

Considering themselves thoroughly biblical, thoroughly Protestant, and thoroughly orthodox, in that order, both of these movements confess themselves to be the standard of Christian truth in the modern world. Both definitely believe in a literal hell. Oddly, however, in spite of their genuine conviction about the reality of retributive punishment, they may have had a part—however small—in hell's "disappearance." More significantly, both groups continue to participate in that loss.

To bring the position of fundamentalism and evangelicalism with respect to hell into clear perspective, this chapter deals first with how each treats forever punishment. Then, secondly, we'll discuss two doctrines that have proved a thorn in the flesh to both groups: "whether salvation is permanent," and "degrees of punishment for evildoers and degrees of reward for the righteous."

Fundamentalism
At the turn of this century, theological liberalism, with its revolt against God, was having a heyday in Protestant circles.

Disbelief in the deity of Christ, rejection of the inspiration of Scripture, and repudiation of eternal punishment were standard planks in the liberal party platform. Here in America, a significant counter-movement developed against liberal theology. Armed with what they called the basic fundamentals of the faith, this movement, known as fundamentalism, clashed in battle with the marauding, renegade liberals.

Under the effective leadership of capable men such as B. B. Warfield, J. Gresham Machen, and James Orr, the fundamentalist movement in its early years had a powerful influence that was felt keenly across traditional denominational lines. A list of the basic fundamentals of the faith was drawn up and stoutly defended. Particular attention was given to the verbal inspiration of the Bible and the deity of Christ and His substitutionary death. And, since universalism was so strongly advocated by the liberal movement, the fundamentalists countered with an equally strong emphasis on the reality of eternal punishment.

Soon, however, the creative leadership in the fundamentalist circle was swallowed up in denominational and academic responsibilities. An anti-intellectualism came into the movement, and many fundamentalists took an almost morbid delight in proclaiming to the wicked their due dessert for sin. Fundamentalism developed a rigid, compassionless legalism that surrounded the whole question of hell. The fundamentalists demonstrated a knack for using the doctrine of hell as a cudgel to club those who resisted their evangelistic advances.

Because of its inherent caustic legalism, this later fundamentalism, as a movement, has not proven a healthy blessing to the church. A significant number of people who today complain that they had too much fire and brimstone preaching when they were young lay this accusation at the feet of "those fundamentalist preachers."

No doubt the fundamentalists have been *a* factor in producing the prevailing mood of indifference and resistance to hell. Yet, in all fairness, it must be acknowledged that the fundamentalists have played a relatively small role in the overall decline of the doctrine.

The stronger of the current crop of fundamentalists do not often preach on hell. Those who accuse them of giving out a diet of nothing but hell and damnation would more than likely not make such a charge—if they listened more carefully.

Evangelicalism

Emerging from a combination of the remnants of the earlier brand of fundamentalism and a reaction against lethargic, mainline Protestant orthodoxy, the modern evangelical movement has risen to prominent and significant proportions in recent decades.

Defying concise definition and not formally organized, evangelicalism crosses denominational lines freely. Its elastic boundaries are determined by each individual who independently chooses whether or not to consider himself an evangelical. Yet at the root, the movement is two-pronged: It is a *theological* movement aiming at a biblical orthodoxy, and it is an aggressive *evangelistic* movement stressing a highly individualistic Christian pietism.

The bulk of theological leadership for evangelicalism is supplied by professors at a number of Christian colleges and seminaries, both denominational and interdenominational. The evangelistic leadership is spearheaded by a variety of parachurch organizations, such as Youth For Christ, Campus Crusade for Christ, World Vision, and Young Life. In addition the influence of evangelist Billy Graham is almost incalculable in terms of providing a degree of visible cohesiveness and exposure to the movement without which it probably would not possess nearly the strength it does.

Evangelicalism's distinctive approaches to theology and evangelism easily collide when it comes to the subject of hell. Biblical orthodoxy, on the one hand, demands a solid belief in the doctrine of eternal punishment. Aggressive, popular personal evangelism, on the other hand, finds a hard line on hell embarrassing and counterproductive in obtaining quick evangelistic decisions.

As a consequence, altogether too many evangelicals have opted for a "pop gospel" in their evangelistic approach. In plain and simple language this means that "sensitive" concepts, such as the serious consequences of sin and hell, though believed in, are astutely avoided in any initial evangelistic presentation. Marked, "not for immediate public distribution," they are set aside for a later time of instruction when they do not pose a threat to the success of an evangelistic endeavor.

I don't intend to suggest here that a positive approach in evangelism is wrong in and of itself. There is certainly no need to bludgeon people with the threat of hell. The problem with the approach of many contemporary evangelicals is that for public image reasons hell is deliberately concealed. It is removed to a safe, innocuous place to insure that the evangelistic presentation remains culturally acceptable. A straightforward treatment of hell hardly qualifies for that. So minimal is the treatment of retributive punishment that its emphasis might be comparable to that of a single, timid piccolo in a hundred-piece brass band. It's there, but it takes a trained ear to pick it out.

Admittedly, it is difficult for me to speak to the issue of hell and evangelicalism because my own heritage is the evangelical movement. It's always most awkward to speak strongly of that from which you've come.

I am not in the least ashamed of the evangelical roots my minister-father gave me. Deep and abiding convictions were built into me as I was growing up, and I have not rejected them—nor do I intend to. But it is those very convictions that are driving me away from the current brand of evangelicalism and ever more closely to the historic church (which is truly evangelical), simply because today's evangelicalism is not keeping the doors closed against the clamor in its ranks for change of its once absolute convictions.

Listening to my sons who play football, I've learned a new word from the vocabulary of a defensive gridiron unit: *contain.* Say the boys, "Contain means to keep your opponent from getting outside of you or invading your flank." Evangelicalism is unable to contain; it has no way of effectively defending its flanks. Having begun in a wholesome purity and having made a constructive contribution to the overall life of the church in America, it now finds no means of purging from its ranks those who do not hesitate to tamper with the historic orthodoxy of the church.

Striking evidence of evangelicalism's inability to *contain,* to maintain a truly orthodox stance, was seen in a recent report appearing in the evangelical publication, *Christianity Today.* The article told of a visit ten evangelicals had with followers of the heretic Sun Myung Moon at the latter's seminary in Barrytown, New York. Summing up the meeting, the report read:

> One evangelical seemed to sum up the sentiments of a number of his colleagues as he offered a farewell comment: "I'm going back and telling everyone I found real Christian fellowship in Barrytown. Of course, I must tell them, too, that many Moonies seem to be following Reverend Moon more than Jesus Christ. But I want you to know that I love you and that I will be praying for you—that the Holy Spirit will convict you of error and lead you to truth. God bless you all."[1]

Such an insipid, sickly reaction to a heretical cult that denies the true divinity of Jesus Christ, that believes He died before He accomplished His true mission, and that believes Sun Myung Moon is the lord of the third advent—the one to accomplish what Jesus failed to achieve—must grieve the overwhelming majority of evangelicals. That an evangelical should affirm Christian fellowship with non-Christians is absolutely mind-boggling. There is no fellowship between light and darkness. Yet evangelicalism has no means to protect itself or its people from the creeping paralysis of such faith-destroying toleration.

---

[1]*Christianity Today* (16 August 1978), p. 41.

Certainly all of evangelicalism hasn't changed—at least not yet. But much of it has. This issue of eternal punishment is one place in particular where unhealthy change has occurred. Many, now apparently ashamed of the preaching on hell done by the classical Protestant preachers who provided evangelicalism's roots, have adopted a new "soft-line" approach.

A 1976 *Christianity Today* article, "Putting Hell In Its Place," provides a typical example of a careless, unchecked "soft line" on hell.[2] Here author Edward Fudge dangerously hedges on the biblical teaching of the degree and extent of eternal punishment.

Admitting there is such a place and that the wicked go there, Fudge sets out with an obvious backhanded slap at great preachers such as Charles Haddon Spurgeon and Isaac Watts. The obvious implication, apparent even from the title of the article, is that these preachers—not hell's critics—removed hell from its proper place.

Then, dismissing these two giants of the past with the all-soothing evangelical shibboleth, "But enough of that; let us look to the Scriptures" (as if Spurgeon and Watts didn't preach the Scriptures!), he makes an incredibly shallow attempt to demonstrate why we should speak of the torments of hell as "aionic" or "new age" instead of "eternal" or "everlasting."

> In our common versions, this word [*aiōnos,* the Greek word for eternal] is usually translated "everlasting" or "eternal." A better translation would probably be the transliteration "aionic" or "new age." *Aiōnos* designates a quality of the Age to Come.[3]

Suddenly, the word *aiōnos* no longer really can mean "everlasting" or "eternal." It's now a quality—whatever on earth, in heaven, or in hell that might be.

In the article, Fudge begins his conclusion with a discussion of this portion of Matthew 25:46, "Then these will go away into

---

[2]Fudge, "Putting Hell In Its Place," p. 14.
[3]Ibid., p. 15.

eternal punishment but the righteous to eternal life.'' Fudge comments:

> Here is ''punishment''—punishment that expresses both wrath and justice. There stands ''life.'' Both terms are rich in meaning for inhabitants of the Present Age. But both are here qualified by the same word ''aionic.'' Both punishment and life are of a quality belonging to the Age to Come and may be described finally only by ''aionic.''[4]

Come on now! This arbitrary tampering with words has gone far enough. ''Aionic'' life *is* everlasting life, not some quality of unknown duration, and ''aionic'' punishment may be described finally only by ''everlasting.'' As I shall show in Chapter 13, where the New Testament Scriptures are dealt with, the word refers to an endless period of time, *not* a quality. Tell me now, who would be excited about having ''aionic'' life and who would be scared of ''aionic'' punishment?

Who on earth knows what ''aionic'' means? Talk about taking the stinger out of hell! Furthermore, there is no way Fudge's shoddy attempt at a linguistic treatment of a handful of Bible verses holds up—as if no Bible expert but him in the last two thousand years caught the ''error'' of using the term ''eternal'' instead of ''new age'' or ''aionic!''

The article's insipid conclusion is shocking, not only that Fudge would write it, but that *Christianity Today* would print it. Wrote Fudge:

> Hell is *one* New Testament picture portraying the fate of the unsaved. But, as we have seen, it is not the only one; *it is not even the primary one. Nor is it the definitive one* [italics mine].[5]

What a far cry this lukewarm stance is from that of the founders of the evangelical movement.

---

[4]Ibid., p. 17.
[5]Ibid., p. 17.

Almost as unbelievable as the appearance of the article itself was the lack of response it received from readers. Only one letter to the editor appeared concerning the article, and that from someone who thought the article was too strong about hell!

Apparently, many who style themselves as evangelicals feel uncomfortable with the biblical doctrine of eternal torment for the wicked. With many evangelicals cushioning or soft-peddalling hell in their message or seeking to change the historic understanding of hell, it is evident that evangelicalism, at least in some quarters, has contributed to hell's going out of style.

Hell and Salvation's Permanence

There are two extremes preached by many fundamentalists and evangelicals that have contributed to the decline in taking hell seriously. Some preach a dogmatic "once saved, always saved" (or perhaps more precisely, "once prayed, always saved") conversion, while others preach that you slip in and out of being saved. Either extreme in its own way can help populate hell.

Let me offer a stern word of caution to both extremes. To pin your hopes upon the doctrines of either airtight eternal security or working to maintain your salvation for your well-being—instead of being found by God under the Lordship of Christ in His church—is playing with fire.

One of my first brushes with the no-security crowd came one summer evening around a campfire where those present were encouraged to testify to their faith in Christ. During the evening a young, light-complected man in his early twenties stood and told how he had just been born again—for the *sixth* time! I thought to myself that it must be one of the counselors pulling a practical joke.

I was wrong!

He went on to tell how five times his willful sins had erased his name from the Book of Life, but that each time he had repented and come back to the salvation of the Lord. *Salvation!* That is no salvation at all. At best, it's an intermittent "maybe." Believing this sort of thing ultimately drives you away from God Himself. People are actually driven towards a hell from which they cannot work up enough meritorious holiness to escape.

In working over the years with high school and college students on both Christian and secular campuses, I have found that the students from holiness backgrounds who are in rebellion against God are some of the most difficult to reach. I have heard them say, "I was doing okay until I committed this sin. I figured, 'What the heck, I've lost it anyway,' so I've gone ahead and blown it all out."

Of course we are after holiness and purity, but not through a perseverance that makes people appeal to their own works and merits for their righteousness instead of to the mercy and forgiveness of God. Discipline, yes! Correction, yes! But both under the protective and watchful care of a strong and gracious church. Do I believe in excommunication? You bet your life! But not where a man unilaterally disqualifies *himself* through guilt. Instead, the Holy Spirit must direct such things under the authoritative voice of the church.

The other extreme comes when people individually decide they are now and forever okay because of personal adherence to a "once saved, always saved" principle.

Almost one hundred years ago the Anglican, E. B. Pusey, in defending the doctrine of eternal punishment, reminded his readers:

> The six sins which are accounted of old to be forerunners of the sin against the Holy Ghost are: "presumption of God's mercy", "obstinancy in sin"; "impenitence"; "despair of salvation"; "impugning known truth"; and "envy at another's grace".[6]

------

[6]*What Is Of Faith As To Everlasting Punishment?* 2nd edition (Oxford: J. Parker, 1880), p. 7.

These ever-pertinent words are appropriate as we briefly consider the implications of the doctrine of eternal security for Christian people.

I was strongly jolted awhile back when a report came of a middle-aged man I know who has left his wife and has become involved in a morally promiscuous life. Ten years ago, this man and his wife (who is also living in adultery) continually had their home open to friends and neighbors for study groups and prayer meetings; they brought many to faith in Jesus Christ.

Recently, when a man of God confronted the adulterer with his sin, the man's eyes clogged up with tears as he said, "Brother, all I can tell you is I know that eternal security is true. That is my hope." *But he would not repent.* There is a declining moral climate in evangelicalism, and this sort of behavior is far too common.

It is true that the orthodox church of Jesus Christ has always taught there is security for those who are in Christ. The Christian man or woman who walks in active, dynamic faith and obedience to Christ in vital union with Him and His people knows the calm, unshakeable assurance of the blessed hope of eternal life.

I know that those who preach and teach eternal security do not for a moment *condone* the sins of fornication, drunkenness, homosexuality, abortion on demand, rape, and the like. But too often this *doctrinal system* seems to assure Christians who persist in such sins that they are still bound for glory on a train to heaven. This makes a mockery of hell and eternal punishment, and mythologizes the warnings of Scripture to believers. The idea that Christians can persist in fornication, homosexuality, and other sins and still be assured of heaven is ridiculous.

Faith in Christ, life in His kingdom, is a dynamic, vital thing. Entrance into God's family is on the basis of His grace and mercy and is because of Christ. And holiness and perseverance are two earmarks of being in the kingdom. That stance brings safety. But for those who are either trying to merit their standing, or who are being cocksure in their unrighteousness, beware: It was our Lord Christ Himself who warned a church whose people had similarly erred, "I will spue you out of my mouth."

Ignorance on Degrees of Reward and Punishment

One more factor to be considered as contributing somewhat to the misplacement of hell is the crucial matter of degrees of heavenly rewards for the righteous, and, correspondingly, degrees of eternal retribution for the wicked. Obscurity or ignorance with respect to degrees of rewards and punishments can do nothing but negatively affect the credibility of the doctrine of eternal punishment. Both fundamentalism and evangelicalism often have failed to make this distinction clear.

Who could possibly believe in the justice of God and at the same time accept the direct teaching, or even the inference, that the murderer of six million Jews and the least offender among all unregenerate sinners will suffer exactly the same punishments in eternal torment? Or is it really any easier to accept the equally preposterous dogma that the most noble of all the saints and the most marginal of all the company of Christians will enjoy identical rewards in the glories of heaven?

Neither idea is taught in the Scriptures, nor is either in the range of the orthodoxy of the church. Both ideas, however, have often been inadvertently perpetuated by adherents of the orthodox doctrines of hell. Not knowing what to say, nothing gets said at all. By default the impression is left that there are no distinctions of rewards and punishments. The result cannot help but be an insensitive attitude of indifference toward both heaven and hell, particularly the latter. It is simply too great a violation of the words of the Bible (to say nothing of the offence of the idea to the justice of God) to advocate, even if it is only by default, such an inadequate view.

Orthodoxy has always recognized degrees of reward and retribution. Even the hell of Dante and Milton acknowledged varying degrees. So do most Protestants, Anglicans, Orthodox, and Roman Catholics. Only a tiny segment of Christendom deliberately insists on across-the-board equality of rewards and punishments. The problem is the lack of clear understanding and teaching in this area.

"Justice" that demands the same penalty for shortchanging a customer at the grocery store by five cents and robbing a bank of five million dollars is "justice" that can't be taken seriously. "Justice" that rewards the loyal, devoted law-abiding citizen in exactly the same way as the one who presses the law to the limit without legal transgression is "justice" that will never excite devotion.

Some base their objection on this variation in punishment or reward on the Lord's parable of the laborers who were hired at different hours of the day but all received the same wages. The point of that parable should not be missed—the boss has a right to pay what he wants. That is, it is a parable of the grace of God.

Now consider the parable of the talents. This one does teach degrees of difference in reward. Or the parable about the servants left in charge of other servants by a departing lord (Luke 12:41-48). You'll recall that in this instance servants left in charge reacted variously to their master's commission to serve, reactions that ranged from beating the other servants to serving them well. The judgments measured out by the master on his return were varied and included cutting certain servants to pieces, beating some with many stripes and others with few stripes, and putting the faithful in charge of all the master's possessions. A heaven and hell where equal rewards or punishments are handed out cannot sustain a belief in them that avoids indifference and callousness toward heaven and hell in general.

And the List Goes On

Our list of reasons for the decline of belief in hell in our time could be multiplied considerably. Modern heretical, non-

Christian cults, such as the Jehovah's Witnesses and the Mormons, fuss against eternal punishment. The psychology-of-religion trip that reduces religion to the realm of experience only has also done its harm, as have many others. But the foremost factors have been considered.

Effectively summing up human efforts to explain hell away, Jonathan Edwards penned these most incisive words:

> All wicked men's pains and contrivance which they use to escape hell, while they continue to reject Christ, and so remain wicked men, do not secure them from hell one moment. Almost every natural man that hears of hell, flatters himself that he shall escape it; . . . But the foolish children of men miserably delude themselves in their own schemes, and in the confidence of their own strength and wisdom; they trust to nothing but a shadow.[7]

No matter how numerous the reasons are for the loss of the truth of hell, nothing about hell, or the danger of it, changes. And in no way will such pitiful excuses avail at the day of judgment.

Eternal punishment for the evil is a fact. The danger to many is great. Kindness demands that the truth be told. Grace insists that the danger be exposed. Mercy cries out for men to be stopped before they end up forever in torment. Platitudes about hell are cruel. Denials of it are lies. Aspersions cast on the character of a God who would punish the wicked are themselves a death sentence to those who hear and receive them.

It is not the preachers of hell who are villains. The true culprits are those who caricature these preachers as such and assure the masses that there is no danger. Nor is there a possibility that a place of eternal torment does not exist. It is a settled fact. God Himself—Father, Son, and Holy Spirit—has spoken it. This is no time to ignore His voice or treat His gracious warning lightly. There is no excuse for anyone ending up in hell. Indeed, the offer of deliverance from hell is as true and sure as the fate of hell itself.

---

[7]*Edwards' Works*, p. 454.

10
The Loud Voice of
Twenty Centuries _____

The Church, the immense bulk of Christendom, has in theory always regarded hell and its concommitants as material facts, and not as merely spiritual experiences. (Such assertions) are made by Irenaeus, Jerome, Athanasius, Thomas Aquinas, Bonaventura, Gerson, Bernard, and indeed by almost all of the Christian Writers.[1]

If there be any doctrine ever taught in the name of Christianity which can claim to be really catholic, it is the doctrine of never-ending punishment. This has been believed by the majority of Christians in all ages, in all Churches, and, with very insignificant exceptions, in all sects. Fathers, Schoolmen, and Reformers, zealous Roman Catholics and ardent Protestants, have agreed that this is an undeniable portion of the Catholic faith.[2]

"But," you may ask, "has the church been consistent on eternal punishment? Has there been agreement in the teaching down through the centuries?"

The answer is yes. As Martin Luther put it in 1532:

Moreover, this article [eternal punishment] has been unamimously believed and held from the beginning of the Christian Church to the present hour, as may be shown from the books and writings of the fathers, both in Greek and Latin languages; which testimony of the entire holy Christian Church ought to be sufficient for us.[3]

---

[1]W.R. Alger, *A Critical History of the Doctrine of a Future Life, vol. 2* (Boston: Roberts Bros., 1878), p. 518.

[2]John Hunt, *Contemporary Review* (April 1878).

[3]Letter to Albert of Prussia. The German text reads: "Zu den so ist dieser

Indeed, it ought to be. But what is the content of that testimony? If we follow the writings of the church from the very beginning on, we will see the fathers believed that there would be a day of judgment on which Christ would separate saved and unsaved, sending the latter to an eternal punishment; and the fathers held consistently to a belief that after death there is no second chance for repentance.

The Ancient Church

Ignatius of Antioch, who may have already been bishop of Antioch in A.D. 70 when Jerusalem was destroyed, left behind several letters to churches written on his way to martyrdom in about A.D. 107. In his letter to the church at Ephesus, this contemporary of many of the Twelve gave a picture of the orthodox teaching on the subject:

> Make no mistake, my brothers: those who corrupt families will not inherit the kingdom of God. Then if those who do this in the flesh are to die, how much more so if by wicked teaching someone corrupts faith in God, for which Jesus Christ was crucified? Such a man becomes filthy and will go to the unquenchable fire as will the man who listens to him.[4]

On his way to death for Christ, Ignatius visited with Polycarp, the relatively young bishop of Smyrna. Some fifty years later the same Polycarp was brought into the arena to face the wild beasts himself. The Roman proconsul attempted to persuade Polycarp

---

Artickel nicht eine lere oder auf satz, ausser der schrift von menschen ertichtet. Sondern klerlich im Evangelio durch helle, reine, ungezweiffelte wort Christi gestifft und gegründet und von anfang der Christlichen Kirchen inn aller Welt bis auf diese stund eintrechtiglich gegleubet und gehalden. Wie das aus weifen der lieben Veter bücher und schrifft, beide, Griechischer und Latinischer sprache. Da zu der teglich brauch und das werck mit der erfarung bis auf diese stund. Welchs zeugnis der gantzen heiligen. Christlichen Kirchen (wenn wir schon nichts mehr hetten) soll uns allein genugsam sien." *D. Martin Luthers Werke,* ser. 1, vol. 30 (Weimar: Kritische Gesamtausgabe, 1883ff.), p. 552.

[4]*Ephesians 16, The Apostolic Fathers,* ed. Jack Sparks (Nashville: Thomas Nelson, 1978), p. 82.

to renounce Christ, threatened him with wild beasts to no avail, and finally said, "I will have you consumed with fire, if you despise wild beasts, unless you change your mind." Polycarp replied: "You threaten fire which burns for an hour and is soon quenched; for you are ignorant of the fire of the coming judgment and eternal punishment reserved for the wicked."[5] Thus the proconsul's threat was opposed by a counter-threat based upon the coming judgment of God—by a man who stood on the threshold of death. Having already given himself up for dead, Polycarp sought only the salvation of his hearer.

But the statements of Ignatius and Polycarp, being incidental to their main concerns, do not give us a complete picture of the ancient doctrine of eternal punishment, and we must go on to other writers for details.

In the latter half of the second century there lived Justin Martyr, a converted pagan philosopher, who wrote in defense of the Christian faith. In his *First Apology,* or defense, he wrote:

> Plato used to say that Rhadamanthus and Minos would punish the wicked who came before them for a thousand years; but we say that the souls of the wicked, being united to the same bodies, shall be consigned over to eternal torment, and not, as Plato will have it, to the period of a thousand years only; but, if you will affirm this to be incredible or impossible, there is no help for you, but you must fall from error to error till the day of judgment convinces you we are right.[6]

To this we may add a statement on the same subject from his *Dialogue With Trypho:*

> At this second Advent of Christ, some will be condemned to suffer eternally in the fires of Hell, while others will be eternally free from suffering, corruption, and sorrow.[7]

---

[5]*Martyrdom of Polycarp* 11, Ibid., pp. 143–44.
[6]Martyr *I Apology* 8.
[7]Martyr *Dialogue With Trypho* 45.

During the second century the greatest defender of Christian orthodoxy was Irenaeus who studied under Polycarp as a youth and became bishop of Lyons. He made it clear that doom of the wicked is not just for a time, nor is it annihilation. In his most famous work, *Against Heresies,* we find eternal punishment mentioned several times for the purpose of converting the reader. For example,

> Thus also the punishment of those who do not believe the Word of God is not merely temporal, but is rendered also eternal. For, to whomsoever the Lord shall say, "Depart from me, ye cursed, into everlasting fire," these shall be damned forever.[8]

He clearly understood that damnation is not an event, accomplished once and ended, but goes on for eternity.

This aspect of the punishment of the wicked gets vivid description in the writings of the North African church teacher, Tertullian (ca. 160-ca.225):

> Therefore after this [the Day of Judgement] there is neither death nor repeated resurrections, but we shall be the same that we are now, and still unchanged—the servants of God, ever with God, clothed upon with the proper substance of eternity; but the profane, and all who are not true worshippers of God, in like manner shall be consigned to the punishment of everlasting fire—that fire which from its very nature indeed directly ministers to their incorruptibility.[9]

Tertullian's strong language meets its match, though, in the statement of Hippolytus of Rome (ca. 170-ca.236), who wrote:

> The fire which is unquenchable and without end awaits these latter, and a certain fiery worm which dieth not, and which does not waste the body, but continues bursting forth from the body with unending pain. No sleep will give them rest; no night soothe them, no death

---

[8]Irenaeus *Against Heresies* IV. 28.2.
[9]Tertullian *Apology* 48.

will deliver them from punishment, nor shall any voice of interceding friends profit them.[10]

Such statements may seem terribly extreme and out of line to the modern mind, but they do indeed express the faith of the church. Cyprian, the great bishop of Carthage who was martyred in A.D. 258, said it well:

> An ever burning Gehenna will burn up the condemned, and a punishment devouring with living flames; nor will there be any time whence they may have either rest or end to their torments. The pain of punishment will be without the fruit of penitence; weeping will be useless, and prayers ineffectual. Too late they will believe in eternal punishment who do not believe in eternal life.[11]

Three Fourth-century Bishops

Clear and uncompromising teaching on hell is reflected in the writing, a century after Cyprian, of Athanasius, the highly renowned defender of the faith who was the instrument for preserving the doctrine of the Trinity during the turbulent fourth century. It was the custom of the bishop of Alexandria to send a pre-Easter letter to the flock, announcing the proper dates and urging them to proper observance. Early in his career as bishop, Athanasius wrote in his Easter letter:

> Therefore the divine word does not allow them to have peace, "For there is no peace to the wicked, saith the Lord" (Is. 48:22). Thus they labor in anguish and sorrow. . . . But such men have the due reward of their folly, since their hope will be in vain because of their lack of gratitude. For there is no hope whatever to the ungrateful. The last fire, prepared for the devil and his angels, awaits those who disregard divine light. Such then is the end of the unthankful.[12]

---

[10]*On the Universe, Against the Greeks and Plato.* The full text of this work is lost to us but a long fragment has been preserved. An English translation of this may be found in *The Ante-Nicene Fathers* (Grand Rapids: Eerdmans, 1956), pp. 221-23.

[11]Cyprian *To Demetrianus* 24.

[12]Athanasius *Third Festal Letter* 2, 4.

Saint Athanasius also pointed ahead to the Second Coming of Christ and the judgment at that time as an occasion of great consequence for the wicked.

From the Scriptures you will learn also of His second manifestation to us, glorious and divine indeed, when He shall come not in lowliness but in His proper glory, no longer in humiliation, but in majesty, no longer to suffer but to bestow on us all the fruit of His cross—the resurrection and incorruptibility. No longer will He then be judged, but rather will Himself be Judge, judging each and all according to their deeds done in the body whether good or ill. Then for the good is laid up the heavenly kingdom but for those that practise evil outer darkness and the eternal fire.[13]

Thus, the picture of the church's position on eternal punishment becomes more sharply focused. Two other fourth-century writers add more clarity. Basil the Great of Caesarea warned the wicked: "Sinners shall be condemned to everlasting punishment, where their worm does not die, and their fire is not quenched."[14]

In the West, Saint Hilary of Poitiers (ca. 367?), the contemporary of Saint Athanasius, when speaking of the final state, said:

Finally, the Apostle warns us beforehand about the end of godlessness, in order to inspire us with the fear of the consequences: "Whose end is ruin . . . but our expectation is in heaven" . . . If the end of the blessed is said to be an expectation, but that of the godless is said to be what is due to them, even in this case we do not believe that the end is their total destruction. For what kind of a penalty will it be for their impiety if they are wholly incapable of escaping the avenging punishments, since through the destruction of their being nothing is found that can feel pain? Consequently, the end is the

---

[13]*On the Incarnation of the Word of God,* English translation (London: A.R. Mowbray & Co., Ltd., 1953), p. 56.3.

[14]*Concerning Faith.* This work may be found in *The Fathers of the Church,* ed. R. J. Deferrari, vol. 9: *St. Basil, Ascetical Works,* trans., M. Wagner (New York: n.p., 1950), p. 64. Basil here quotes Mark 9:43.

perpetual perfection of an unchanging state that is reserved for blessedness and prepared for impiety.[15]

Chrysostom, Augustine, and the Creeds

Shortly after the time Basil and Hilary wrote, the most eloquent John Chrysostom, bishop of Constantinople, penned these words:

> It is necessary that those who have sinned shall put on immortality, not however for any honor to themselves, but in order that the path of that punishment may survive unceasingly. . . . Neither will any severity of torment destroy the soul, nor will the body be able, in that time, to be consumed by burnings, but distressed it will survive with the soul, nor will there be any end.[16]

Nor dare we omit a statement by Augustine, whose writings have been more widely read in the West than those of any other church Father. He repeatedly warned sinners of the perpetual death lying ahead, saying in one place:

> Christ in one and the same place, and in one and the same sentence, said, The wicked shall go away into everlasting punishment; but the righteous into life eternal. If both are eternal, verily either both ought to be understood as long-continuing with an end, or both as perpetual without an end. For they are related as equal to equal, and to say in this one and the same sense, life eternal will be without end, but punishment eternal will have an end is absurd.[17]

But we do not need to rely only on the words of individual teachers in the church. The creeds of the church have always spoken of the return of Jesus Christ to judge the living and the dead. Often, however, especially when there was a need to do so in the fight against heresy, further information was added. Thus,

---

[15]"The Trinity," *The Fathers of the Church,* vol. 25 (New York: The Fathers of the Church, Inc., 1954).

[16]Chrysostom *To Theodore after his Fall* I. 10.

[17]Augustine *The City of God* 21.23.

Irenaeus prepared a creed for his time, which he said represented the faith of the church. It reads in part:

> . . . that, according to the good pleasure of the Father invisible, every knee of those that are in heaven and on the earth and under the earth should bow before Christ Jesus, our Lord and God and Savior and King, and that every tongue should confess to him and that he may execute righteous judgment over all: sending into eternal fire the spiritual powers of wickedness, and the angels who transgressed and apostasized, and the godless and unrighteous and lawless and blasphemous among men, . . .[18]

Nevertheless, we do not find eternal punishment to be an article in any of the creeds that came out of the Seven Ecumenical Councils, held between A.D. 325 and A.D. 787. There is a very good reason why: Those councils dealt with matters of faith that were in dispute. This one was not. Very few people in those days questioned the doctrine of eternal punishment.

Among all the creeds of Christendom there are three that rank highest, indeed one, two, three in this order: the Apostles', the Nicene, and the Athanasian. Though the last was not authored by Athanasius, it came into wide use in the church around the seventh century. Always highly regarded in the church, it must be given great weight. It closes:

> Those who have done good will enter eternal life, and those who have done evil will go into eternal fire. This is the true Catholic faith. Unless a man believe this firmly and faithfully, he cannot be saved.

Beginning with the time of the Reformation, we find many of the creeds giving attention to the destiny of the wicked. The following list will make this graphically clear.

---

[18]Irenaeus *Against Heresies* I. 10.1.

Whatever Happened to Hell?

Creed	Statement on Eternal Punishment
Augsburg Confession (1530)	Our churches also teach that at the end of the world Christ will appear for judgment and will raise up all the dead. To the godly and elect he will give eternal life and endless joy, but ungodly men and devils he will condemn to be tormented without end.
The Orthodox Confession of the Eastern Church (1643)	Question 121: (Response) . . . All souls shall return to their own bodies and receive in them the perfect and eternal reward of their deeds and actions, but the bodies of the wicked also will be imperishable because they are to be tormented with eternal punishment.
The American Congregational Creed (1883)	We believe in the ultimate prevalence of the kingdom of Christ over all the earth; in the glorious appearing of the great God and our Savior Jesus Christ; in the resurrection of the dead; and in a final judgment, the issues of which are everlasting punishment and everlasting life.
The Belgic Confession of Faith (1561)	. . . the terrible vengeance which God shall execute on the wicked, . . . who shall be convicted by the testimony of their own consciences, and, being immortal, shall be tormented in that everlasting fire which is prepared for the devil and his angels.
The First Confession of Basel (drafted by Oecolampadius, revised by Oswald Myconius) (1534)	We believe that there will be a Day of Judgment on which the resurrection of the flesh will take place, when every man will receive from Christ the Judge, according as he was lived in this life: eternal life, if out of true faith and with unfeigned love he has brought works of righteousness which are the fruit of faith; or everlasting fire if he has

112

Creed	Statement on Eternal Punishment
	done either good or evil without faith or with a feigned faith without love.
The Scottish Confession of Faith (1560)	On the other hand, the reprobate and unfaithful departed have anguish, torment, and pain which cannot be expressed.
The Second Helvetic Confession* (1566) *Composed by Heinrich Bullinger, it became the most widely received among Reformed confessions.	But the unbelievers and ungodly will descend with the devils into hell to burn forever and never to be redeemed from torments.
Westminster Confession (1646)	. . . but the wicked, who know not God, and obey not the gospel of Jesus Christ, shall be cast into eternal torments, and be punished with everlasting destruction from the presence of the Lord, and from the glory of his power.
The Dordrecht Confession (Mennonite-Anabaptist) (1632)	And that, on the contrary, the wicked or impious shall, as the accursed of God be cast into "outer darkness;" yea, into eternal, hellish torments; "where their worm dieth not, and the fire is not quenched;" and where—according to Holy Scripture—they can expect no comfort nor redemption throughout eternity.
New Hampshire Baptist Confession (1833)	We believe that the end of the world is approaching; that at the last day Christ will descend from heaven, and raise the dead

Creed	Statement on Eternal Punishment
	from the grave to final retribution; that a solemn separation will then take place; that the wicked will be adjudged to endless punishment, and the righteous to endless joy; and that this judgment will fix forever the final state of men in heaven or hell, on principles of righteousness.
Statement of Fundamental Truths, Assemblies of God	Whosoever is not found written in the Book of Life, together with the devil and his angels, the beast and the false prophet, will be consigned to everlasting punishment in the lake which burneth with fire and brimstone, which is the second death.
The Mennonite Confession of Faith (1963)	He will deliver the kingdom to God the Father, cleanse the world by fire, create new heavens and a new earth, consign unbelievers to eternal punishment, and usher His children into the eternal bliss of the world to come.
Creed of the Huria Kristen Batak Church (1951)	Those who do not believe, however, will go to everlasting torment.

Thus, we can see why Philip Schaff, summing up the agreement of all Christendom in eight general categories (which he calls "The Catholic Consensus of Greek, Latin, and Evangelical Christendom" gives as his eighth and final category:

Eschatology
1. Death in consequence of sin
2. Immortality of the soul
3. The final coming of Christ
4. General resurrection

5. Judgment of the world by our Lord Jesus Christ
6. Heaven and Hell. The eternal blessedness of saints and the eternal punishment of the wicked.
7. God all in all (I Cor. 15:28)[19]

Indeed, what more needs to be added? Is there the slightest room for doubt as to where God's people have stood on the issue of hell? We surely have established here that which we stated at the beginning: The church has indeed taught clearly that at the consummation of the ages, all will appear before Christ for judgment; and the wicked, those who finally departed this life scorning Him, will be sent into an eternity of punishment.

[19]*Creeds of Christendom,* vol. 1 (New York: Harper, 1877), p. 921.

115

11
Chinks in the Armor _____

Is there not even one crack in the armor—one ray of hope for the wicked? Isn't there someone who has taught something different about hell? Wasn't there a famous man named Origen who way back in history taught that there is no such thing as eternal doom?

Attacks on the Doctrine of Eternal Punishment

Origen (ca. 185-255) is indeed known for his rejection of an ultimate and perpetual punishment for the wicked. His theory on this matter sprang from his wild speculations concerning the preexistence of souls set forth mainly in his book, *First Principles*.[1] There he posited a view that all souls were originally intellectual existences. These existences weren't exactly creatures, and they didn't have bodies. All of them were created by God and were equal. They could think and act, and they had the power of free will. They fell from their original unity as pure rational spirits, and the world we live in is a result of the disunity produced by their fall. Wild, isn't it?

Obviously, the source for Origen's ideas on origins is the pagan Greek philosopher, Plato, who also taught a similar preexistence of souls. Origen developed his own system, however, for he had a bent toward creativity, a feature that must be used carefully by those who aspire to be theologians. His account of the overall plan of the ages was most fascinating while at the same time radically different from anything the church had ever taught. For

---

[1]*First Principles*, trans. G.W. Butterworth (New York: Harper & Row, 1966).

our purposes here, it is enough to know he taught that the material universe we experience came into being because some intellectual existences departed from their original goodness. In plain language this means that the physical universe is the result of evil done by these supposed intellectual "things." The various forms of plant, animal, and human life were given to different ones as punishment, so that they ultimately could be restored to their original states.

This restoration of all fallen intellectual existences to their original states is to be accomplished, said Origen, through the creation and existence of numerous worlds and ages until God, somehow, will become all in all. Even the devil himself will be restored and will participate in the kingdom of God. Obviously, there can be no eternal punishment for mankind in a system where everyone, even the devil, ends up in the glories of heaven,

How did the church respond to this teaching? His own bishop, Demetrius of Alexandria, excommunicated Origen.

This bishop held two councils, A.D. 231 and 232, against the great theologian and enacted that he, for his false doctrine, his self-mutilation, and his violation of the church laws, be deposed from his offices of presbyter and catechist, and excommunicated.[2]

That council was followed and upheld by one held by Pontian, bishop of Rome. Most of the bishops of Christendom did likewise, but Origen found a home in Caesarea where the bishop, unfortunately, allowed him to teach. Therefore, the writings of this brilliant heretic continued to cause the church much trouble. In the late fourth century (A.D. 399), three councils were held at Alexandria, Jerusalem, and Cyprus specifically to anathematize Origen and his views.[3] In A.D. 553, the Fifth Ecumenical Council, the second of Constantinople, condemned Origen and published

[2]Philip Schaff, *History of the Christian Church* (Grand Rapids: Eerdmans, 1962), p. 789.
[3]Karl Joseph Hefele, *History of the Councils,* vol. 2 (New York: AMS Press, 1972), pp. 418–19.

fifteen anathemas against him, dealing specifically with his views on eternal punishment and "restoration."[4] As if this were not enough, the Seventh Ecumenical Council, the second of Nicea, also condemned him and his views.

Individually, Jerome and Epiphanius were outstanding fourth-century opponents of Origen and his philosophical humbug. Jerome wrote: The Bishops of Rome, Alexandria, Milan, Aquileia, and the whole Synod of Catholics, both of East and West, with a like sentence, because their mind is alike, denounce Origen to the people as a heretic."[5]

Augustine and Vincent of Lerins also were fourth- and fifth-century enemies of the views of Origen; and the emperor Justinian, theologian as well as ruler, was a strong sixth-century opponent. Indeed, it was Justinian who wrote: "If anyone says or thinks that the punishment of demons and of impious men is only temporary, and will one day have an end, and that a restoration will take place of demons and of impious men, let him be anathema."[6]

So much for Origen. Anyone who takes refuge in him as one who taught against eternal punishment takes refuge in a heretic and cannot be said to be pronouncing the views of the church. Let us not, therefore, call him up as a witness that the doctrine of eternal punishment is optional.

But are there not others? "Oh yes," someone will say, "did not the church Father Gregory of Nyssa teach that all will be saved? What of him?"

It is true that Gregory did follow Origen in some of his writings. In one of his works there are references to the eventual cleansing of the wicked, the eradication of evil, and the restoration of

[4]Henry R. Percival, *The Seven Ecumenical Councils* (New York: Edwin S. Gorham, 1901), pp. 314–19.
[5]Jerome Apology II. 22.
[6]Percival, *The Seven Ecumenical Councils,* p. 320.

everything, including the devil, to God.[7] Nevertheless, in a work written *four years after* the one loved by the universalists, Gregory sounded quite different. Of the last judgment he wrote that God will give to each his due; repose eternal to those who have exercised piety and a holy life; but the eternal punishment of fire for the harsh and unmerciful. And to the rich who have made a bad use of their riches, he thundered, "Who will extinguish the flames ready to devour you and engulf you? Who will stop the gnawings of a worm that never dies?"[8] It seems that the universalists should be more reticent in claiming Gregory as their father.

For many centuries there was no controversy at all concerning the doctrine of the eternal destiny of the wicked. Even John Hick, certainly no friend of orthodox Christianity, concedes that the view of the final state of man that Augustine held "dominated the imagination of the West for the next thousand years and more."[9] Thus, during the Middle Ages, there were few defectors to universalism. Scotus Erigena (?–880) did revive Origen's teachings, but his own writings were condemned. And even in Erigena's framework the worst people suffered eternal punishment.

Attacks from the Fringes of Christianity

In the sixteenth century, at the time of the Reformation, certain of the groups called "Anabaptist" began to propound various novel doctrines. A formal council of certain Anabaptists, held in Italy in 1550, included in its ten points of agreement, "There is no hell but the grave."[10] Such doctrines were jumped on by the Reformers. Article XVII of the Augsburg Confession reads, "Rejected, therefore, are the Anabaptists who teach that the devil and condemned men will not suffer eternal pain and torment."

---

[7]Gregory *The Soul and the Resurrection,* vol. 5.

[8]Gregory *About Loving and Embracing the Poor in Kindness* II. The Greek text is in J. P. Migne, *Patrologia Graeca* 46, pp. 472-89.

[9]*Death and Eternal Life* (London: Collins, 1976), p. 198

[10]Earl Morse Wilbur, *A History Of Unitarianism: Socinianism and its Antecedants* (Boston: Beacon Press, 1965), pp. 84-85.

During the fifteenth and sixteenth centuries, as a by-product of the Renaissance, editions of Origen's works were published, and it seems likely that these and the revival of interest in Platonic thought had a major influence on the controversies involving eternal torment that arose in the seventeenth century.

One of the more important groups involved in those controversies consisted of the followers of Faustus Socinus. These antitrinitarians, called Socinians, taught that instead of being tormented forever, the wicked would just be annihilated.[11] Apparently, they hoped that by eliminating the offensive concept of God's tormenting people forever, they would gain followers. Thus, in an account by Valentin Schmalz, detailing a colloquy they held at Rakow in 1601, we find these words:

> The dead are reduced to nothing; the body disappears, the spirit returns to Him who gave it, that is God. The soul feels neither pleasure nor pain. And thus, since the form of their life and their life has perished, they are all wholly non-existent.[12]

Though it seems likely that even among themselves the Socinians were divided on this issue, the church at large rose to the occasion and burning denunciation fell upon these views from all corners of Christendom. Romanists, Arminians, Calvinists, and Lutherans all rose to the defense of the orthodox doctrine. Socinian works on the subject received very little circulation, and the annihilationist doctrine did not gain a foothold in Christendom.

But other attacks were to come. In England there were, in the mid-seventeenth century, a number of Arians (people who believed that Christ was not God) who did not believe in eternal punishment. Their attempts to promote their doctrines were, however, quickly refuted by churchmen. As Nicholas Chewney

---

[11]Ibid., pp. 77–80

[12]Quoted in Ibid., p. 86. D. Cantimori and E. Feist, *Per la Storia degli Eretici Italiani del secolo XVI in Europa Lesti. . .* (Rome: Reale accedemia d'Italia, 1937), pp. 249–53.

put it, the church saw their views as, ". . . an old Origenian Heresie new vampt [to piece something old with a new part] on the Socinian last."[13]

From another quarter, however, a small group of intellectuals began to make an impact. D. P. Walker writes, "John Locke, Isaac Newton, Samuel Clarke, and William Whiston all knew each other. All were Arians and all disbelieved in eternal torment."[14] Whiston became the major spokesman for their point of view—one held by a number of other "reasoning men" of their day. This ideology suggested that there was a limited period of torment for the wicked followed by their annihilation. Actually, the argument by Whiston is not particularly well reasoned. He and his friends just simply believed that a loving God would never torment anyone forever. In the end, as is so often the case with universalists, rationality bowed to emotion, and Whiston waxed hot on "barbarous cruel opinions inconsistent with the Love of God."[15]

Some of the English Arians were men of note, and waves of shock rippled through the church. Many orthodox churchmen were especially angered by the fact that Whiston and his friends liked the heretics, Origen and Arius, while hating the great orthodox Father, Athanasius. Whiston's writings in particular drew a number of replies, some of them the clearest statements in the English language of the orthodox doctrine of life after death.[16] Though one critic, Horbery, worried about the effects of Whiston's writings and said, ". . . by denying the Perpetuity both of Reward and Punishment, he has done, perhaps more than any Man living to destroy the comfort of good Men, and hinder the

[13]D. P. Walker, *The Decline of Hell* (London: Rontledge and Kegan Paul, 1964), p. 93.

[14]Ibid.

[15]William Whiston, *The Eternity of Hell Torments Considered* (London: n.p., 1740).

[16]For example, Matthew Horbery, *An Enquiry into the Scripture Doctrine Concerning the Duration of Future Punishment* (London: n.p., 1744).

121

Repentance of the Wicked,''[17] the church was not deeply shaken, and true doctrine held.

Meanwhile a different breed of heresy was making the rounds in England. Arianism, which denies the true divinity of Christ, often carries with it a denial of complete redemption and a denial of eternal punishment. All through the seventeenth century Arians of various stripes were popping up here and there. Among them were Englishmen deeply affected by the revival of interest in the writings of Plato.

Two such men were Peter Sterry and Jeremiah White.[18] Both were mystics, and they were close friends, though White was almost twenty years the younger. In their writings we find the usual concern about vindicating God from the dishonor of sending most people into eternal torment. Their system included preexistence of souls, universal salvation, and the restoration of all things. God's love was their overwhelming theme, and hellfire was that love burning the sins out of the wicked: "God himself puts forth himself immediately and naked upon them at once to torment them, and also to sustain them in their Torments. . . O! who can express the riches of the Joy and Glory of those Spirits. . ."[19] Quite a switch!

Naturally, one would expect to find lovers of Origen among Platonists. Thus, there was published (anonymously) in 1661, *A Letter of Resolution concerning Origen and the Chief of his Opinions,* perhaps written by George Rust, a Platonist who had become Bishop of Dromore. The *Letter* contained Origen's system in its entirety including preexistence of souls and the restoration of all living beings to God. Again, the church labeled these ideas as novelties, and the controversy they stirred certainly did not make people forget hell. However, this and other Origenist works kept universalism alive well into the eighteenth century.

---

[17]Quoted in Walker, *Decline of Hell,* p. 103.

[18]Ibid., Chapter VII.

[19]Jeremiah White, *Restoration of All Things,* 3rd edition (London: John Denis & Son, 1789), pp. 226–28.

Still another line of universalism was being developed in England. Anthony Ashley Cooper, third Earl of Shaftesbury, wanted a religion without rewards or punishments. He argued that there are two reasons why men obey God: ". . . either in the way of his power, as presupposing some disadvantage or benefit to accrue from him; or in the way of his excellency and worth, as thinking it the perfection of nature to imitate and resemble him."[20] Shaftesbury wanted no self-serving religion, but a totally disinterested one in which we do what is good just because it is good. This concept was to be picked up by later universalists.

Meanwhile, several men on the European continent were teaching universal salvation and denying the eternal doom of the wicked. One such was Johann Wilhelm Petersen, who had been dismissed from his post as Lutheran Superintendent of Lüneburg because—having become convinced that the millennium was coming soon—he had preached universal salvation in the churches. Since this doctrine had been condemned along with Origenism in the Augsburg Confession, his dismissal was only a matter of course. He formed a group who repeatedly had spiritual revelations, and this group soon hooked up with an English group of Platonic, Origenistic mystics. Heretics have strange bedfellows, and it was not long before there was a "revelation" that salvation was universal and punishment limited. Soon Petersen published a defense of this new doctrine—in three volumes![21] Naturally, he connected the doctrine with his notion that he was living in the last days; indeed the time was ripe for the true doctrine of universal salvation to be believed. Peterson was intelligent and very knowledgeable, and thus was able to put together every conceivable historical quote to support his views. A storm of protest arose, and many refutations of Petersen's doctrines were published—certain proof that eternal judgment was not a dead issue.

---

[20]Walker, *Decline of Hell,* p. 168.
[21]J. W. Petersen, *Mysterion* (n.p., 1710).

It is most interesting to note that Petersen, similar to most universalists of his age, was not willing to give up punishment entirely. He did not like the potential social results of freedom from fear of God's punishment of the wicked. Thus, unrepentant sinners, by his system, had to expect thousands of years of punishment.

Although they made some ripples, these seventeenth- and eighteenth-century opponents of the doctrine of eternal punishment still stood on the fringes of Christianity.

Attacks from Within the Visible Limits of the Church

In eighteenth-century England, universalism was debated heavily, particularly because of the influence of the respected mystical devotional writer, William Law, who published the concept of universal salvation held by the radical pietists in Germany. Law fell under the influence of Jacob Boehme and went from him to other mystical writers. Eventually he came up with a temporary hell to cleanse the wicked: "As for the purification of all human nature either in this world or in some after-ages, I fully believe it."[22]

John Wesley, in expressing abhorrence of Law's doctrine of a purgatorial hell, exclaimed: "If there be no unquenchable fire, no everlasting burnings, there is no dependance on the Scriptures. No Hell, no Heaven, no revelation."[23]

It was in the mid-eighteenth century that unitarian-universalism began to receive a formal group of adherents. David Hartley published his *Observations on Man* in 1749 in which he expounded his ideas about the future life. These ideas included a limited future punishment:

> If there be no Punishment in another State, besides what is absolutely eternal, Men of very low Degrees of Virtue will hope to escape

---

[22]William Law, *Letters 191.*

[23]Stephen Hobhouse, *Selected Mystical Writings of William Law* (London: The C. W. Daniel Company, 1940), p. 351

this, and consequently to escape with Impunity; Whereas, if there
be a purging Fire, into which all the Wicked are to be cast to remain
and suffer there according to their Demerits, far beyond what Men
will generally suffer in this Life and if there be only a few, that are
admitted to Happiness after the Expiration of this Life, without such
future Purification; what Vigour and Earnestness should we use to
escape so great a Punishment, and to be of the happy Number of
those whose Names are written in the Book of Life.[24]

Hartley's hell, like Law's, was a type of purgatory, meant to
draw men back to good. When Joseph Priestley adopted
Hartley's scheme, the early direction of Unitarianism was set. In
America, King's Chapel in Boston became Unitarian in doctrine
in 1785. Priestly moved to America and in 1796 started a
Unitarian Society in Philadelphia. Parenthetically, we might add
that another "denomination" formed in independent-minded
America, the Universalists, sprang from basically the same roots
and eventually joined the Unitarians. In spite of their claims that
people are turned away from God by the doctrine of eternal
punishment, it is interesting to note that neither group ever com-
manded a large following. Future decades were to see numerous
disputes about eternal punishment (more than any other issue)
between Christians and Unitarians. As you would expect, those
who defended orthodoxy held that God's punishment of the
wicked expresses His abhorrence of sin. On the other side, the
Unitarians insisted that punishment had the purpose of reforming
and that a loving God simply could not do otherwise.

All of this harks back to one's concept of the nature of God. As
noted earlier, many who oppose the idea of eternal punishment
do so because of their view of God. John Kentish, writing in 1798
gave a perfect example of the typical hard-line Unitarian statement:

Pure, unlimited benevolence is, in our judgment, the most glorious
perfection of the Divine character. We believe, according to the

---

[24]Geoffry Rowell, *Hell and the Victorians* (Oxford: Clarendon Press, 1974),
p. 37

> language of the favourite Apostle, that "God is Love"; we consider
> all his moral excellencies, his justice, truth and holiness, as modifi-
> cations of this principle. Happiness we regard as the grand object of
> his works and dispensations and conceive of his glory as resulting
> from the diffusion of this happiness.[25]

Thus, that same defective doctrine of the nature of God with that inadequate concept of sin are again the root of this eighteenth- and early nineteenth-century Unitarianism. Its advocates are blind to all but "benevolence" as "love" and to all but "love" as the nature of God. Sin is simply not seen as being all that monumental. Their whole system is materialistic and mechanistic, which reflects a desire to make God in their own image. Accordingly, since they do not want eternal punishment to exist, the God they create must feel the same way. As a consequence, pointed out Charles Jerram, an evangelical preacher of the day, their sermons had ". . . no unction in them; no appeal to conscience; no instruction for the poor, if such had constituted part of their assembly; no consolation for the afflicted."[26]

Other kinds of universalists also plagued the nineteenth century. One of the most influential in the intellectual world was the German theologian, Friedrich Schleirmacher, who formulated a subjective theological system reminiscent of Origen. Schleirmacher, often called the father of modern Protestant liberalism, wrote, "Through the power of Redemption there will result in the future a general restoration of all human souls."[27]

Still another influential writer was the Scotsman Thomas Erskine, who had read the later works of William Law and had

[25]J. Kentish, *The Moral Tendency of the Genuine Christian Doctrine* (1798), p. 11 (quoted in Rowell, *Hell and the Victorians,* p. 45.)
[26]Rowell, *Hell and the Victorians,* p. 50.
[27]*The Christian Faith,* ed. H. R. MacKintosh and J. S. Stewart (New York: Harper & Row, 1963), p. 722.

been impressed by his arguments for universalism. Erskine wrote:

> I trust that He who came to bruise the serpent's head will not cease his work of compassion until he has expelled that fatal poison from every individual of our race. I humbly think that the promise bears this wide interpretation . . . in fact my soul refuses to believe in final ruin, when it contemplates the blood of Christ."[28]

In that statement can be seen a strong difference between the universalism of the Unitarians and that of Erskine. The Unitarians claimed to base theirs on reason; he based his on his own individualistic interpretation of the Scriptures. One of his greatest concerns was the possibility that anyone should believe that good works held any promise at all of a future reward. He believed that the righteousness of God was communicated to all men who only needed to appropriate it (shades of Karl Barth!). Man didn't need to try to become righteous by good works. Confusing the regenerated man with men in general, he, like Origen, believed in the restoration of all men to God. John Henry Newman, later to be a cardinal, found these views to be so contrary to orthodoxy and so influential that he wrote tracts against them.

But the nineteenth century produced not only universalists as disbelievers in eternal punishment. F. D. Maurice, who many claim was not a universalist, deposed professor at King's College, London, did not believe in a universal restoration; but, as we have seen, he hated the idea of eternal torment and hoped that all men would be saved. Thus, he wrote in his *Theological Essays,* "What, then, is Death Eternal, but to be without God?"[29] Though his writings have been characterized as cloudy, he did believe that the punishment of the wicked consisted in being left alone by God. A Wesleyan reviewer pointed out that, "If this is

---

[28]Rowell, *Hell and the Victorians,* p. 71.
[29]*Theological Essays,* 3rd edition (London: Macmillan, 1853), p. 437.

the true doctrine, not only the peasant and the beggar, but the cold-blooded murderer, the brutal ravisher, the most fiendish of slavedrivers of all the children of the devil on earth, and all the demons of hell, may 'rejoice and sing merry songs' together."[30] Fenton John Anthony Hort, coauthor of a Greek New Testament called the *Wescott-Hort Greek Testament,* corresponded with Maurice, however, expressing agreement with the idea that the power of repentance is not limited to this life.[31]

Counterattack

Among the great defenders of orthodoxy in the nineteenth century were the so-called Tractarians, including E. B. Pusey, John Henry Newman, Henry Manning, H. P. Liddon, and J. M. Neale. The movement started with a revival of orthodoxy begun by a sermon on national apostasy by John Keble in July, 1833. The men involved spoke strongly on life after death. Indeed, their sermons, tracts, expositions, and hymns formed a more than adequate answer to the Unitarians and universalists.

A clear example of Pusey's preaching and teaching may be found in an 1839 message:

> Be this then ever before us; be our first thought morning by morning to think of the morning of the resurrection; be our last night by night, the sleep of death, after which cometh the judgment . . . remember the parching flame, the never-dying worm, the ever-lasting fire, the gnashing of teeth, "the smoke of torment" which "goeth up for ever and ever"; where they have no rest day nor night. Set heaven and hell before your eyes, so you may escape hell, and by God's mercy attain heaven.

Despite the fact that in 1864 eleven thousand English clergy signed a declaration affirming that the punishment of the wicked

---

[30]Rowell, *Hell and the Victorians,* p. 83.
[31]A. F. Hort, *Life and Letters of F.J.A. Hort,* vol. 2 (London: Macmillan, 1871), p. 266.

is everlasting,[32] both in Europe and the Americas, the nineteenth century saw a relaxation in the doctrine. By the end of the century few preachers were willing to emphasize the doctrine of eternal punishment. By and large even those who believed in it, as most did and probably still do, were unwilling to debate men such as F. W. Farrar who did not believe that the fate of man was "finally and irrevocably sealed at death."[33]

Farrar's book, *Eternal Hope,* excited more popular interest in the nineteenth century than any of the other heretical writings on this topic. In his book, *Mercy and Judgment,* he declaimed eloquently:

> I would, here and now, and kneeling on my knees, ask that I might die as the beast that perish, and forever cease to be, rather than that my worst enemy should endure the Hell described by Tertullian or Minutius Felix or Jonathan Edwards, or Dr. Pusey, or Mr. Furniss, or Mr. Moody, or Mr. Spurgeon, for one single year.[34]

For those who would hear, however, an able and definitive answer came from the eighty-year-old E. B. Pusey, still contending for the faith in his old age. He reminded Farrar that the strongest and hardest teaching on the eternal condition of the wicked comes from Christ. A poem quoted by Pusey sums up the facts:

> Christ on Himself, considerate Master, took
> The utterance of that doctrine's fearful sound:
> The Fount of Love His servants send to tell
> Love's deeds: Himself reveals the sinner's Hell.[35]

---

[32] Rowell, *Hell and the Victorians,* p. 121.

[33] F. W. Farrar, *Eternal Hope* (New York: E. P. Dutton & Co., 1881), p. 86.

[34] F. W. Farrar, *Mercy and Judgment* (New York: E. P. Dutton & Co., 1881), p. 485.

[35] E. B. Pusey, *What is of Faith as to Everlasting Punishment,* 2nd edition (Oxford: J. Parker, 1880), p. 47. Also used by Pusey in Letter IV, *Theological and Ecclesiastical Subjects,* "Spiritual Letters of E. B. Pusey," ed. J. O. Johnston and W. C. E. Newbolt (London: Longmans, 1898), p. 137.

12
Hell and the Old Testament _____

Tales of the fate and place of the departed dead fill the literature of antiquity. Virgil and Homer took their epic heros to the realm of the dead and then back again to tell about it. Fanciful and frightening were the details these adventurers related upon return to the land of the living.

One collection of ancient literature dealing with the departed dead, however, stands out uniquely from all the rest: The Old Testament. Though its great characters made no epic voyages to the place of the dead to gain firsthand knowledge of the world to come, it describes the future of the dead with the ring of absolute authority and a gravity not found in any other ancient source. The elements of myth, fancy, and hopelessness are utterly lacking in it. Instead there is a positive declaration of what is to come after death for both the wicked and the righteous. In it there is despair and doom for the godless, but a confident expectation of blessedness for the faithful. Who among us is not familiar with the last phrase of the beloved Twenty-third Psalm, "And I will dwell in the house of the Lord forever."

Blindly, some critics of hell have charged that the Old Testament view of the fate of the dead is crude and obscure. Even the casual reader will easily judge for himself that this is not true. I will happily grant that the New Testament is much clearer than the Old Testament on the subject of eternal punishment. That is surely to be expected. The same is true of salvation, the Incarnation of the Son of God, heaven, and almost all other subjects common to both Testaments. Simply because the New Testament is more comprehensive than the Old Testament in its treatment of hell does not mean the latter is crude and unclear. There is much to gain from an examination of Old Testament data on the fate of the unrighteous dead.

Sheol

The crucial issues surrounding eternal punishment in the Old Testament revolve around one key word: *Sheol*—the name of the place of the dead. Once the use of that word is understood, we will have a clear perception of retributive punishment under the old covenant.

The Meaning of Sheol

Our key word *Sheol* is no rarely-used word in the Old Testament; it appears sixty-four times. Most up-to-date English translations of the Bible render that word *Sheol* as "Sheol." That is, they bring it straight over from the Hebrew into English without any change. Older English translations sometimes render it as *hell* and at other times, appropriately, *grave,* as do all modern English translations. Occasionally, even *pit* is used in translation. The King James Version, for example, has *grave* thirty-one times, *hell* thirty-one times, and *pit* three times.

The word *Sheol* can by no means stand for the place of eternal punishment every time it is used in the Old Testament. Sometimes it does; sometimes it doesn't. *Grave* is often the intended meaning, in the same way we use the word in everyday English. For instance, "He was buried in a new grave."

So how do we know in a given Scripture whether *hell* or *grave* is meant? There can be an eternity of difference between those two words, but the context is quite adequate to clarify the meaning in the majority of cases. Just to get a feel for it, look at an example or two of each of these major usages. Jacob, mourning the reported death of his son, Joseph, said to his sons and daughters, (as reported in Gen. 37:35) ". . . 'Surely I will go

131

down to Sheol in mourning for my son.' " Jacob was not saying here, "Surely I will go down to the place of eternal torment mourning for my son." Obviously that was not to be Joseph's final destination.

Then there is Job who cries out to God when answering the charges of his three accusing friends, "Oh that Thou wouldst hide me in Sheol, That Thou wouldst conceal me until Thy wrath returns to Thee . . ." (Job 14:13). It would be ridiculous to understand Job's meaning to be, "Oh that Thou wouldst hide me in hell, that Thou wouldst conceal me until Thy wrath returns to Thee. . . ." Hell is not the place to be hidden from the wrath of God. It is the place where the wrath of God is experienced. Job's meaning here is, "Hide me in the grave until your present wrath is past." We'd be more likely to say it like this: "Just let me drop dead until this whole thing is over."

There are dozens of other places in the Old Testament where "grave," as the place of all the dead, is clearly the meaning of the word *Sheol*. But the idea of the grave, even if considered as the common abode of the dead, both good and evil, is totally inadequate to be the meaning intended in many, many other references.

One clear illustration of the usage of *Sheol*, where it cannot mean the grave, is found in Psalms 9:17: "The wicked will return to Sheol, even all the nations who forget God." If *Sheol* as used here were to be considered the common final abode of both the good and the bad, the whole point of the passage would be lost. What threat would there be to the wicked? The preceding verse reads, "The LORD has made Himself known; He has executed judgment. In the work of his own hands the wicked is snared" (Ps. 9:16). The context here is the judgment of the wicked—both present and future. The notion that the wicked are punished by consignment to the same neutral grave as the righteous is as foreign to Scripture as is the idea that there is no reward whatever for the righteous. When "the wicked return to Sheol . . .," they go to that place of misery reserved solely for the evil.

The Jews of Old Testament times were well aware that there was life after death with rewards for the righteous and punishment for the wicked. Many Old Testament Scriptures speak pointedly about it. Consider Deuteronomy 32:21,22:

> They have made Me jealous with what is not God; They have provoked Me to anger with their idols. So I will make them jealous with those who are not a people; I will provoke them to anger with a foolish nation, For a fire is kindled in My anger, And burns to the lowest part of Sheol, And consumes the earth with its yield, And sets on fire the foundations of the mountains.

There is no way *Sheol* could mean simply "grave" in this passage. Who could imagine God saying here that His anger would burn to the seventy-first inch of a six-foot grave? Neither would there be any meaning to having His fire burn to the lowest level of a grave for all the dead, good and evil. *Sheol* here is beyond question a reference to a place of punishment for the evil.

I have seen pompous claims by some that the Old Testament reveals no future punishment, and that Sheol is the expectation of the wicked and the righteous alike. A claim like that wilts as a rose in the light of Old Testament Scriptures, such as the one we have just examined. And there are others. For example:

> As sheep they are appointed for Sheol;
> Death shall be their shepherd;
> And the upright shall rule over them in the morning;
> And their form shall be for Sheol to consume,
> So that they have no habitation.
> But God shall redeem my soul from the power of Sheol;
> For He will receive me (Ps. 49:14,15).

And,

> Thou wilt make known to me the path of life;
> In Thy presence is fulness of joy;
> In Thy right hand there are pleasures forever (Ps. 16:11).

133

Plainly, simply, and clearly, the Old Testament here draws a sharp distinction between the destiny of the righteous and the unrighteous. The place of the righteous provides forever blessing. The place of the unrighteous provides forever misery.

True, the full terms of the distinction are not as clear as they will be by the time we've read all through the New Testament to Revelation 22:21. But such an eternal division with respective misery for the wicked and blessing for the righteous is evident in the Old Testament, and the Jews of that covenant understood it with a fair degree of comprehension. God spoke to the people of old Israel and declared that there would be punishment forever for the evil and blessing forever for the righteous.

Only a century ago biblical critics were dogmatically asserting that the Jews in more ancient Old Testament times had no idea of such a life-after-death program. They maintained no one on the whole earth did. Thus they concluded that centuries later other Old Testament writers inserted these "new notions" of eternal punishment into the older texts to make it appear that such a belief had always been held.

Today, no reputable scholar would dare question the antiquity of such understandings. It has been demonstrated beyond doubt that not only did ancient Israel believe in life after death with blessing or punishment, but so did other ancient peoples such as the Egyptians. But such is life for the unbelieving biblical critic. His conclusions are so short-lived.

Sheol as the Place of Eternal Punishment

It is reasonable to ask, "Why does the word *Sheol* have a double meaning? We don't use the English word *grave* to double for eternal punishment. Why is *Sheol* used for both?"

Remember those tedious dictionary exercises back in elementary school? You learned then that words are commonly called on for more than one meaning, but that those meanings are often related. Such is the case with *Sheol,* doubling both for the grave and the place of everlasting misery for the unrighteous.

An example of some other related English words will help clarify this. Consider the words *die* and *death:* "To cease to live; become dead; decease." Or, "To suffer spiritual death." That's how the dictionary defines *die*. In the same vein *death* is said to mean, "Cause or occasion of loss of life," and "Cessation or privation, as of function, existence, capacity for development, etc.; extinction." But there are places in Scripture where different meanings, not wholly out of keeping with these definitions, are demanded for the two words.

Examples abound, but only a few are needed to illustrate the point. God, speaking through the prophet Ezekiel, declared, "But when I say to the wicked, 'You will surely die,' and he turns from his sin and practices justice and righteousness, . . . he will surely live; he shall not die" (Ezek. 33:14,15). Even as *to live* is here the reward of the righteous, so *to die* is here plainly the punishment of the wicked. It is impossible in this instance to limit the meaning of *to die* to the experience of expiring in this life. Both the wicked and the righteous expire. But *to die* here means to enter that state of punishment for the unrighteous that comes after death in this life, and this punishment is in bold contrast to the reward for the righteous.

Similarly, Paul speaks of death beyond death when he says, "For the wages of sin is death, but the free gift of God is eternal life in Christ Jesus our Lord" (Rom. 6:23). And John did the same when he wrote, " '. . . He who overcomes shall not be hurt by the second death' " (Rev. 2:11). Again, and yet even stronger, John said, "And death and Hades were thrown into the lake of fire. This is the second death, the lake of fire" (Rev. 20:14). *Die* and *death* are employed in these three Scriptures to refer to the eternal punishment of the ungodly. There is no imaginable way to limit that punishment merely to the stillness of physical death. There is hurt and torment in this dying after dying, in this death after death.

After seeing how these words are often used in Scripture, it is no problem to understand why *Sheol* sometimes means "grave" and sometimes "the place of everlasting punishmment of the ungodly." The word falls in the same category as the words *die* and *death*. Surely the reference point of Sheol is often merely the grave just as *death* often means to expire in this life. But there are times when that *grave* is the same as that death after death, the death which is torment. *Death* and *Sheol* commonly appear together in that sense. In Proverbs 5:5,6, we read of an adulterous woman, "Her feet go down to death, Her steps lay hold of Sheol. She does not ponder the path of life; . . ."

Commenting on the appropriateness of the double use of Sheol, William T. Shedd, the nineteenth-century theologian, said:

> Sheol signifies the "grave", to which all men, the good and the evil alike go down. That Sheol should have the two significations of hell and the grave, is explained by the connection between physical death and eternal retribution.[1]

Were *Sheol* to always mean the physical grave, the threats of death for the wicked would be utterly pointless because the righteous would be receiving the exact same threat. That is not what is being suggested. The righteous are not threatened or punished for being righteous.

Without doubt, then, *Sheol* is often the word used in the Old Testament for that tormenting death after death—that grave beyond the grave. The word is thoroughly appropriate and repeatedly speaks of what comes after our last breath in this life. Limiting the meaning of Sheol to a sod grave will never do. Wouldn't the unrighteous person delight if the punishment for his unrighteous life was limited to a hole in the ground! But according to the Old Testament that is far from the truth. The grave indeed awaits the ungodly, but that grave is far more than a hole in the ground in which a body decays. Beyond that grave is *the* grave, hell, with its endless woe.

---

[1]*Endless Punishment* (New York: Charles Scribner's Sons, 1886), p. 34.

Sheol and All Its Old Testament Meanings

When a Jew under the old covenant saw or heard the word *Sheol,* what did he understand? What mental pictures did that word present? The answer to these questions will greatly aid our understanding of the word's use and meaning in Old Testament times as well as during Jesus' day.

Six facets of meaning come to mind.[2]

1. *No One Ever Comes Back*

The Old Testament reveals that people who went to Sheol went with a one-way ticket. No one ever came back. Job showed that in his terse reply to the agitating Eliphaz:

"When a cloud vanishes, it is gone,
So he who goes down to Sheol does not come up.
He will not return again to his house,
Not will his place know him any more" (Job 7:9, italics mine).

The most forlorn of human myths speak of those places from which it is said, "None shall return." Humanity holds deep within its bones the fear of unending separation from all that is known and loved. Thus, many of the heroic epics end with the triumphal return of one who has conquered the evil place and come home to tell about it. The tragedies end with mourning for the brave and adventurous hero who died attempting the impossible. These tales are heartrending, and noble, but they do not come close to conveying the cold, stark terror that Job's simple words must bring: "He who goes down to Sheol does not come up."

---

[2]For the basic headings in this section I am indebted to Moses Stuart, *Future Punishment* (Philadelphia: Presbyterian Publication Committee, 1867), pp. 159 ff. This work on the subject of eternal punishment is outstanding. Though it was well known in its day, I have found no opponent of the doctrine of endless punishment who successfully replied to Stuart. It is unfortunate that all of Stuart's work was not consistent with the orthodox faith. Thoroughly sound on the retribution of the wicked, he erred greatly in the more important areas of doctrine relating to the Incarnation of the Son of God. Perhaps it is for this reason that Stuart is seldom read today even though his work on the subject under consideration here is excellent.

Don't shrug off the strength of this simple statement, because this time it is not a myth or an heroic tale. It is the reality of the separation of the wicked person from all that he has known and cherished, all that is good and beautiful. He vanishes into the place of terror and dread, and you won't see him again.

This dim view of Sheol goes well beyond the physical fact of being buried in an earthen grave. The undesirable world of another sphere of consciousness is in view here. The Old Testament knows no permanent termination of consciousness for anyone. Consciousness continues after physical death, but in a vastly different place. One in Sheol is as fully conscious as one on earth—perhaps more so. The dirt grave itself was merely part of the transition to a different sphere of consciousness, the entrance to a vast domain reserved for those departed from this life. There was no coming back.

2. *A Place of Unending Conscious Deterioration*

As sheep they are appointed for Sheol;
Death shall be their shepherd;
And the upright shall rule over them in the morning;
And *their form shall be for Sheol to consume,*
So that they have no habitation (Ps. 49:14, italics mine).

So said the psalmist of the foolish ones who trusted in earthly riches to secure themselves eternally. These thought money would provide them a home forever, but they will be forever with no home. On top of that, Sheol will forever nibble away at them; it will endlessly consume them. Can you fathom it? This homelessness and consuming takes place in a ceaseless existence.

I remember my own thoughts of heaven and hell when I was in my teens. I certainly did not want to end up in hell. But quite frankly, I wasn't all that "keyed up" about heaven either. Ceaseless existence was the reason. I could see that hell was bad, but a ceaseless existence anywhere seemed almost as bad. My understanding of life after death was extremely foggy. But an endless *homelessness,* an eternity of deterioration—with no hope of either ever coming to an end—how unbelievably awful.

3. *The Place of Conscious Silence and Boredom*

In Sheol the evil are totally severed from fellowship with God, from any contact with Him whatever. In anguish David cried out:

> Return, O Lord, rescue my soul; Save me because of Thy lovingkindness. For *there is no mention* [or *rememberance*] *of Thee in death;* In Sheol who will give Thee thanks? (Ps. 6:4,5; italics mine).

It's all over between the sinner and God in Sheol. There is no memory of Him; there is no praise of Him. ''The dead do not praise the LORD, Nor do any who go down into silence; But as for us, we will bless the LORD From this time forth and forever . . .'' (Ps. 115:17,18). What a contrast! The morose silence of Sheol against the praises of the Lord forever.

Sheol is the place of estrangement from God, the region of nonrelationship with Him or anyone. It is the realm of eternal, self-centered loneliness. This is conscious silence and boredom, the epitome of the ''dull life,'' multiplied to the infinite power. Warns the wise preacher, ''. . . there is no activity or planning or wisdom in Sheol where you are going'' (Eccles. 9:10).

Normally, my father's method of punishing me when I was a child was the yardstick. But occasionally he employed the sit-on-a-chair-for-an-hour method. Oh, do I remember how slowly the hour passed, especially when I could hear my friends playing outside. The dullness and boredom of one idle hour is hard to describe. Multiply all the silence, dullness, and boredom you've ever known or thought of by eternity and square it. Then you'll begin to get an inkling of this Old Testament concept of Sheol being a place of conscious silence and boredom for the wicked dead.

4. *The Opposite of Heaven*

Whatever heaven is, Sheol is its opposite. And the opposite of heaven is hell. David's often-sung and read Psalm on God's "everywhereness," Psalm 139, vividly and dramatically pictures this:

> Where can I go from Thy Spirit?
> Or where can I flee from Thy presence?
> If I ascend to heaven, Thou art there;
> If I make my bed in Sheol, Thou art there.
> (Ps. 139:7,8)

Sheol here is not the physical grave of a dead man. It is the realm of the dead beyond the grave; it is the antithesis of heaven.

And speaking of the unavoidable judgment of God and those who would seek to escape it, Amos the prophet said:

> "Though they dig into Sheol,
> From there shall My hand take them;
> And though they ascend to heaven,
> From there will I bring them down" (Amos 9:2).

Sheol is the farthest one can get from heaven.

5. *Pitch Black and Gloomy*

The complaining Job, mistakenly feeling he was under the heavy hand of the judgment of God, moaned:

> "Would He not let my few days alone?
> Withdraw from me that I may have a little cheer
> Before I go—and shall not return—
> To the land of darkness and deep shadow;
> The land of utter gloom as darkness itself,
> Of deep shadow without order,
> And which shines as the darkness" (Job 10:20–22).

This fate is reserved for those under God's judgment among whom Job felt compelled to class himself at this point in his troubles. Darkness, gloom, deep shadow without order—shining as the darkness. That is anything but a pleasant scene.

Have you ever been in a forest on a black, silent night when even the light of the sky was hidden behind the clouds? You could feel a heavy, oppressive darkness. The darkness was brilliant and the silence could be heard. So Job described his feeling of Sheol.

Life at its worst on this side of the grave is infinitely superior to that black death in the land of eternal night that is so intense it shines as the darkness. A moment of cheer in this life is a veritable oasis compared to such horrible darkness from which there is no return.

6. *Sheol Is Sometimes Personified*

Compassionless and without pity is the monster Sheol. "Therefore Sheol has enlarged its throat and opened its mouth without measure" (Isa. 5:14). It is never satisfied, no matter how many it takes in, "Sheol and Abaddon [the place of perishing] are never satisfied . . ." (Prov. 27:20). It takes its prey alive and whole: "Let us swallow them alive like Sheol, Even whole, as those who go down to the pit" (Prov. 1:12).

Surely, Sheol does not have an actual consciousness. But as sure as death itself, the power of darkness wrestles to bring in all it can to share its doom and gloom.

Conclusion

Far from lacking a concept of a place of eternal retribution for the wicked, the Old Testament pictures Sheol as a place to be avoided at all costs. And under the old covenant, mankind was not left alone between two passive, neutral choices—heaven and hell—to choose at leisure which one might be preferred. A battle rages between active, vested powers. Both aggressively seek all men, one to bring them to life, joy, and peace with God and all the heavenly hosts; the other to drag men down to the horrors of hell to share the fate of its prince.

A final, forever devouring, silent, purposeless, most distant place from God's heaven, shining with darkness and gloom, seeking all it may devour—that is the picture of the place of eternal punishment as it was understood by the people of the Old Testament.

It would be foolish to claim that the Old Testament revelation regarding eternal punishment is as clear as that of the New Testament. But it is evident that those under the old dispensation were vividly aware that not only was there an eternal life and reward for the righteous, but there was an eternal death and retribution for the ungodly.

13
Hell and the
New Testament

Although the Old Testament case for eternal punishment is conclusive enough, the New Testament teaching on it is even more definitive. So lucidly clear is it that no man or woman of right mind who hears or reads the facts in Scripture could possibly be justified in doubting the overwhelming seriousness of hell. Propriety and discretion demand that any suggestion contrary to the awesome and fearful reality proclaimed by God with respect to eternal damnation for the unrighteous give way hastily to the truth of what He has spoken. As Paul once said, ". . . let God be found true, though every man be found a liar . . ." (Rom 3:4). That same type of exhortation was offered by Martin Luther in a letter he wrote in 1522:

> . . . one must separate widely our way of thinking from God's truth, and take care that we do not make God a liar, but far rather allow that all men, angels and devils will be damned than that God should not be truthful in His words.[1]

If you look at the Words of God, you will see why the church has consistently made the same interpretation of them.

The Bottom Line
After every Scripture has been examined, every orthodox creed considered well, and the opinions of orthodox theologians taken into account, one issue stands as far more basic than all

---

[1]Walker, *Decline of Hell*, pp. 7–8.

others combined: *What did Jesus say?* All else in the Bible about eternal punishment must be understood and interpreted in the light of what He said. He is, after all, *the* final authority.

Nothing any human could write to explain Jesus' words could be as clear and powerful as His own words. Therefore, let me bring to your attention the great majority of the words of Jesus that bear unequivocally and directly on the subject of eternal punishment. I've put them together consecutively, though not chronologically, so that the overwhelming clarity and power of them cannot be missed. Let them sink deeply into your heart. I hardly think, having done so, any who follow Him as Lord would then dare to say there is no hell. (Italics in these verses are mine.)[2]

"But when the Son of Man comes in His glory, and all the angels with Him, then He will sit on His glorious throne. And all the nations will be gathered before Him; and He will separate them from one another, as the shepherd separates the sheep from the goats; and He will put the sheep on His right, and the goats on the left. . . . Then *He will also say to those on His left, 'Depart from Me, accursed ones, into the eternal fire which has been prepared for the devil and his angels;* . . . *And these will go away into eternal punishment,* but the righteous into eternal life" (Matt. 25:31–33,41,46).

"And if your hand causes you to stumble, cut it off; *it is better for you to enter life crippled, than having your two hands, to go into hell, into the unquenchable fire.* And if your foot causes you to stumble, cut it off; it is better for you to enter life lame, than having your two feet, to *be cast into hell.* And if your eye causes you to stumble, cast it out; it is better for you to enter the kingdom of God with one eye, than having two eyes, to be *cast into hell, where their worm does not die, and the fire is not quenched"* (Mark 9:43–48).

"For what does it profit a man to gain the whole world, and *forfeit his soul?"* (Mark 8:36; cf. Luke 9:25).

"Now it came about that the poor man died and he was carried away by the angels to Abraham's bosom; and the rich man also died and

---

[2]Note: I have relied heavily on the arrangement of texts from Shedd, *Endless Punishment,* pp. 15–17.

was buried. And *in Hades he lifted up his eyes, being in torment,* and saw Abraham far away, and Lazarus in his bosom" (Luke 16:22,23).

"And do not fear those who kill the body, but are unable to kill the soul; but rather *fear Him who is able to destroy both soul and body in hell"* (Matt. 10:28).

"The Son of Man will send forth His angels, and they will gather out of His kingdom all stumbling blocks, and those who commit lawlessness, and will *cast them into the furnace of fire; in that place there shall be weeping and gnashing of teeth"* (Matt. 13:41,42).

"Many will say to Me on that day, 'Lord, Lord, did we not prophesy in Your name, and in Your name cast out demons, and in Your name perform many miracles?' And then I will declare to them, 'I never knew you; *depart from me you who practice lawlessness"* (Matt. 7:22,23).

"And whoever shall speak a word against the Son of Man, it shall be forgiven him; but whosoever shall speak against the Holy Spirit, *it shall not be forgiven him either in this age, or in the age to come"* (Matt. 12:32).

"You serpents, you brood of vipers, how shall you escape *the sentence of hell?"* (Matt. 23:33).

"But if that slave says in his heart, 'My master will be a long time in coming,' and begins to beat the slaves, both men and women, and to eat and drink and get drunk; the master of that slave will come on a day when he does not expect him, and at an hour he does not know, and will *cut him in pieces, and assign him a place with the unbelievers"* (Luke 12:45,46).

"He who has believed and has been baptized shall be saved; but *he who has disbelieved shall be condemned"* (Mark 16:16).

"So it will be at the end of the age; the angels shall come forth, and *take out the wicked from among the righteous, and will cast them into the furnace of fire; there shall be weeping and gnashing of teeth"* (Matt. 13:49,50).

"Do not marvel at this; for an hour is coming, in which all who are in the tombs shall hear His voice, and shall come forth; those who did the good deeds, to a resurrection of life, *those who committed the evil deeds to a resurrection of judgment*" (John 5:28,29).

Does any question remain as to whether or not Jesus declared the eternal punishment of the wicked? All the authority of the almighty God is present in the Words He spoke about hell. Jesus had more to say about hell than any other speaker or writer in the Bible. If He was mistaken in what He said, then the almighty, eternal, and everlasting God was mistaken. And that is not the case. Indeed, if it comes to a disagreement: "Let God be true and every man a liar." Even the universalist, John A. T. Robinson, admitted:

It is futile to attempt to prove Christ taught no belief in hell or eternal punishment, though much, it is true, may, and must be said, by way of modification.[3]

What more could Jesus have said?

There is absolutely no way the clear impact of His words can be brushed aside, and the assertion made that there is no eternal doom for the ungodly, unless of course, we join the critics who arbitrarily determine that Jesus didn't really say these things at all. But if such a foolish choice were to be made, we would have departed from Christianity in favor of some modern fictitious, man-made religion. There is no other Christianity than that which Jesus Christ established. And His Christianity clearly, distinctly, emphatically, and even threateningly speaks of a very real hell. Those who maintain Jesus did not utter these severe sayings about hell are like gamblers playing a game they will surely lose.

---

[3]"Universalism—Is It Heretical," *Scottish Journal of Theology* (June 1949), p. 154. It is apparent Robinson sees the consequences of his admission. Being a universalist, he is forced to make the illogical conclusion he does about modification in the latter part of the statement.

Five New Testament Words on the Wicked

A clear meaning of Jesus' words about hell can be gained from an examination of five pertinent words used in relation to it. These words are: *Hades, Tarturus, Gehenna, forever,* and *eternal.* If you deal with these words there is little room for misunderstanding what is involved in the future punishment of the wicked. The first three will be considered in this chapter, the last two in the next.

1. Hades

The word *Hades* is Greek and was used by other peoples in the ancient world. Homer, the Greek poet, had his Ulysses going down into Hades on one occasion. The Roman poet, Virgil, at one point described Aeneas's progress in the regions of Hades. For the Greeks and Romans, Hades was the world of all the dead, both good and evil. Located in the very bowels of the earth, it was a happy place for no one. How grimly the Greeks saw it can be sensed in the words of the dead Achilles (he had become a chief in Hades) as he responded to the visiting Ulysses' effort to comfort him by bringing to mind his former greatness:

> Renowned Ulysses! think not death a theme
> Of consolation; I had rather live
> The servile hind [farmhand] for hire, and eat the bread
> Of some man scantily himself sustained,
> Than sovereign empire hold o'er all the shades
> [departed spirits].[4]

The Hades of the Greeks and Romans was sullen and dull. At its best it was far from being as pleasant as the former life had been at its worst. It was divided into sections with each section having its own relative degree of misery. One's place in Hades was determined by how he had lived before his death. The whole of Hades was deep, dark, and gloomy with no hope whatever.

---

[4]Robert Southey, ed., *The Works of William Cowper,* vol. 14 (London: Baldwin and Cradock, 1837).

It was this Greek word *Hades* that those who translated the Hebrew Old Testament into Greek chose to use for the Old Testament word *Sheol* in almost every case.[5] It happened to be the most convenient and closest word available in the Greek language.

Hades is used ten or eleven times in the New Testament, and without doubt it refers to the exact same place as *Sheol* does in the Old Testament. There is one interesting difference, however. In the New Testament *Hades* is never used to mean simply a sod grave; its only use is to describe the place of retribution for the wicked.

Jesus' parable of the rich man and the beggar, Lazarus, contains the most powerful and illuminating use of Hades in the New Testament:

> "Now it came about that the poor man died and he was carried away by the angels to Abraham's bosom; and the rich man also died and was buried. And in Hades he lifted up his eyes, being in torment, and saw Abraham far away, and Lazarus in his bosom. And he cried out and said, 'Father Abraham, have mercy on me, and send Lazarus, that he may dip the tip of his finger in water and cool off my tongue; for I am in agony in this flame.' But Abraham said, 'Child, remember that during your life you received your good things, and likewise Lazarus bad things; but now he is being comforted here, and you are in agony. And besides all this, between us and you there is a great chasm fixed, in order that those who wish to come over from here to you may not be able, and that none may cross over from there to us' " (Luke 16:22–26).

These were not the words of some ill-informed, unlearned child of his time. They came from One who is fully God and fully man. Jesus gave us here a cutaway view of what exists beyond the grave. Recognizable beings are there—the rich man, Lazarus, and the long-deceased Abraham. The rich man actually recog-

---

[5]I refer here to the Septuagint.

nizes Abraham and calls him by name. These beings are not merely invisible spirits, as we are so prone to think of the departed dead. Indeed, they left their physical bodies on this earth. Yet beyond the grave, but before the resurrection, Abraham has a bosom on which the poor man, Lazarus, no longer poor, can lean. And the rich man has a tongue that can feel the heat of the flame where he's at.

I do not pretend to understand all that these things mean. Is the flame there identical to the flame of a blast furnace in Pittsburg? Are the visible forms of the people made of the same stuff as are our bodies here on this earth? Who, besides God, knows for sure? But one thing is sure: Whatever these flames and forms are, they are real. There are real voices and real words, real agony and real comfort. There are no wings and harps for the righteous, but there is happiness.

Also, absolutely astonishing in this preview of the afterlife is the proximity of the evil and the righteous, and the fact that the evil could see the righteous, and that some communication between the two was possible.

Equally amazing is the extremely definite and final distinction between the two abodes, a distinction firmly fixed by an impassable gulf. There was no going over from one side to the other. There was no second chance for the wicked.

Generally, Hades, the place where the rich man found himself, has been understood in the church to be the abode of the unrighteous dead until the resurrection of both evil and good. You will recall the words of Jesus mentioned above:

"Do not marvel at this; for an hour is coming, in which all who are in the tombs shall hear His voice, and shall come forth; those who did the good deeds, to a resurrection of life, those who committed the evil deeds to a resurrection of judgment" (John 5:28,29).

The torment of the ungodly does not wait to begin until that resurrection. It begins upon physical death and occurs in Hades, the intermediary abode of the unrighteous dead between physical

149

death and the general resurrection of the dead.[6] There is actual torment and suffering in Hades, but Hades itself is not, as such, the place of eternal punishment. John gave further light on this in the Revelation. At the time of general resurrection (referred to also in John 5:28,29) he saw that

> . . . the sea gave up the dead which were in it, and death and Hades gave up the dead which were in them; and they were judged, every one of them according to their deeds. And death and Hades were thrown into the lake of fire. This is the second death, the lake of fire. And if anyone's name was not found written in the book of life, he was thrown into the lake of fire (Rev. 20:13-15).

Both Hades and its inhabitants will end up in the place of eternal torment, the lake of fire. What change, if any, this will make in Hades, Scripture does not reveal.

Is there an intermediary abode for the departed godly? That is not as easy a question to answer. Concerning one point, however, there is no question. The departed of God's people went to paradise. The words of Jesus to one of the two malefactors crucified with Him, ". . . today, you shall be with Me in Paradise," come to mind as soon as the word *paradise* is mentioned. That was the dwelling place of the parabolic Lazarus and the very real Abraham.

Paradise was the intermediary abode of the righteous, at least until the Resurrection and Ascension of Jesus Christ. Many feel that paradise ceased to be after the Resurrection and Ascension of Jesus. Scriptures such as ". . . When He ascended on high, He led captive a host of captives. . . ." (Eph. 4:8), and, "we are of good courage, I say, and prefer rather to be absent from the body and to be at home with the Lord" (2 Cor. 5:8), appear to support

---

[6]Hades, as the intermediary abode of the unrighteous, carries with it no idea of purgatory. Neither the Roman church nor any others who maintain a doctrine of purgatory confuse the two or identify the two as being the same.

that conclusion. Others feel the "paradise program" is still in effect. The church has granted more latitude here than with Hades. The historic church does, however, agree that whether the departed believer is in paradise, or heaven itself (if there is a difference), he is present with the Lord in a place of great blessing and happiness. Hades or Sheol, on the other hand, is the present place of punishment of the wicked.

Regrettably, there are those who would attempt to discredit Christ, the Bible, and the church by insisting that because of the use of the word *Hades,* the whole idea of Hades was borrowed from paganism by early Christianity. That is followed by the assumption, "Of coure, now that we've matured, we need to reject it completely as paganism itself." No plausible support can be given to such an idea.

When a Greek word was needed to render the Hebrew *Sheol,* it would have been meaningless to make up a new Greek word. But that does not demand that the meaning of *Hades* remain absolutely identical to that of the Greeks.

Many a Greek word underwent considerable change in meaning when called upon to do duty in the New Testament. The word *theos* (from which we get our word theology), for example, was taken from Greek and used in the New Testament to refer to God almighty, but that does not demand a Greek view of the gods for our God. Who would be so foolish and blasphemous as to charge that the idea of God was borrowed from paganism because the Greek word *theos* is used for God? The word *agape* was taken for love, but a dimension of definition was given to it of which the Greeks had no knowledge or experience. The word *Hades* gets its definition from how it is used in Scripture, not from Virgil or other pagan sources.

2. Tarturus

The apostle Peter used an expression involving hell that appears only once in the whole New Testament. In context it is extremely illuminating on the subject of the judgment of God and ensuing punishment, so I give it in full.

> But false prophets also arose among the people [in the Old Testament], just as there will also be false teachers among you, who will secretly introduce destructive heresies, even denying the Master who bought them, bringing swift destruction upon themselves. . . . and in their greed they will exploit you with false words; their judgment from long ago is not idle, and their destruction is not asleep. For if God did not spare angels when they sinned, *but cast them into hell* and committed them to pits of darkness, reserved for judgment; . . . then the Lord knows how to rescue the godly from temptation, and to keep the unrighteous under punishment for the day of judgment, and especially those who indulge the flesh in its corrupt desires and despise authority . . . (2 Pet. 2:1,3,4,9,10; italics mine).

The expression of interest here is "God . . . cast them into hell." There is actually no noun in the Greek New Testament text for the word *hell* in this statement. The verb *tartaroō,* which means "to send or cast into Tarturus," is used. The translation, "cast them into hell," is quite proper, however.

Tarturus is another Greek expression almost identical in meaning to Hades. Tarturus was, in fact, the lowest spot in the Greek Hades. Peter wanted an expression that would show the degree of judgment passed by God on angels who sinned. Translated into modern English, he said, "God cast them to the very bottom of hell." The meaning can hardly be mistaken.

It is silly and pointless to argue, as some seem to feel obliged, that the Greek Tarturus was only an imaginary place. Therefore, Peter spoke ignorantly of an imaginary place he mistook for real. (I'm sure the ones who Peter described there wish it were only imaginary!) Peter gave the word *real* content.

There is a second issue of great consequence to be noted in Peter's statement, "to keep the unrighteous under punishment for the day of judgment." Punishment for the ungodly is forever, and it begins before the final judgment. In some instances it begins even in this life.[7] But in all cases the unrighteous are kept under punishment in Hades from the moment they die. Later that punishment continues in the eternal lake of fire.

3. Gehenna

Hades and *Tarturus* are powerful words indeed, but there is one that is stronger yet—*Gehenna*. It is the ultimate in terms of severity. The word appears twelve times in the New Testament, and with only one exception (see James 3:6), Jesus is the only One who uses it.

Used in its primary, literal sense, Gehenna is the Valley of Hinnom, located just south of Jerusalem. Its history is horrid and ugly. Ahaz and Manasseh, two of the most wicked kings ever in Israel, offered their own sons as burnt offerings to the idol-god, Moloch, in this place. From the words of the Lord through Jeremiah the prophet, it is apparent this practice spread far beyond the kings themselves, for against Israel God charged:

> "And they have built the high places of Topheth, which is in the valley of the Son of Hinnom, to burn their sons and their daughters in the fire, which I did not command, and it did not come into My mind" (Jer. 7:31).

Topheth, one of the names given to the Valley of Hinnom, means "the place of burning." According to the ancient rabbis, the idol, Moloch, was hollow inside, and after being heated with fire, little children were laid in its arms and veritably roasted alive. What an abominable place this was for Israel! So much so that "abomination" became another meaning for Topheth. In time even a more harsh meaning came to be associated with Topheth—"to vomit with loathing." Gehenna, the Valley of Hinnom, Topheth, they all speak of the same geographic location—the most detestable place in all Israel.

So awful was this notorious place that the good King Josiah "defiled Topheth" (2 Kings 23:10). That is, he made it the gar-

---

[7]Cf. Romans 1 where the wrath of God is experienced as a this-life reality.

bage dump of Jerusalem. That was hundreds and hundreds of years before Christ, and it was still the city dump in His day. The foul offal of the city was disposed of there. Perpetual fires necessarily burned at Topheth, or Gehenna, to consume the garbage deposited. It was a place of filth and putrefaction, infested with worms and accompanied with an unbelievable stench. Jesus' hearers would not have wondered why He described the Gehenna of eternal punishment as that place "where the worm dieth not, and the fire is not quenched." Worms, filth, and fire had been the fare for that valley for centuries.

It defies the imagination to think of a place worse than Gehenna. Any Jew who had seen it, even without knowing its historical background, would have no difficulty understanding why Jesus would use the word to refer to the most loathsome place in all existence.

Understandably then, Gehenna, in its secondary sense, is hell. It is *the* place of retributive suffering, the place of fire and brimstone, the lake of fire, the place of the eternal torment of those condemned because of unrighteousness. It is the everlasting abode of the devil, his angels, and those whose names are "not found written in the Lamb's book of life."

Though Jesus is the only one in all the New Testament to use Gehenna in this specific sense, He was not the first to use the word to signify the place of eternal torment. Evidence abounds that Gehenna had carried that meaning for more than a century before Christ. Joachim Jeremias remarked, ". . . the Valley of Hinnom came to be equated with the hell of the last judgment in apocalyptic literature from the second century B.C."[8] The people were anything but bewildered by Jesus' use of the word when He spoke of being cast into the Gehenna of fire (Matt. 18:9). None of His listeners imagined He literally meant the Jerusalem garbage

---

[8]Gerhard Kittel, *Theological Dictionary of the New Testament,* ed. and trans. Geoffrey Bromily (Grand Rapids: Eerdmans, 1964–1976).

dump, though probably all who had seen or heard of it called the mental picture of that to mind. It was clear to everyone that He meant the place of eternal torment for the wicked.

Hell has come under popular ridicule in recent times because of the idea of unquenchable fire. We are told bizarre preachers have used the imagery purely for emotional effect. Those with such a complaint, however, are going to have to lodge it against Jesus Christ Himself. It is none less than He who makes that unquench-able fire so plain, ugly, terrifying, and inescapable in His teaching on hell. He is the One in Scripture who introduces the unquench-able, eternal fire of Gehenna to be associated with eternal tor-ment.

Likewise, Jesus is the One who makes Gehenna the ultimately bad place to go. To the scribes and Pharisees He said, " 'You serpents, you brood of vipers, how shall you escape the sentence of hell [Gehenna]?' " (Matt. 23:33).

Prior to His sending the twelve disciples on a missionary ven-ture, He warned them regarding those who would oppose them violently:

> "And do not fear those who kill the body, but are unable to kill the soul; but rather fear Him [God] who is able to destroy both soul and body in hell [Gehenna]" (Matt. 10:28).

There is nothing more final for the wicked than Gehenna.

John, the beloved apostle of Jesus, did not use the word *Gehenna* when he wrote the Revelation. But beyond question, Gehenna is there. The very place Jesus called Gehenna is spoken of when, concerning the destruction of the beast and the false prophet, John wrote:

> And the beast was seized, and with him the false prophet who performed the signs in his presence, by which he deceived those who had received the mark of the beast and those who worshipped his image; these two were thrown alive into the lake of fire which burns with brimstone (Rev. 19:20).

Whatever Happened to Hell?

And of the devil himself he said:

> And the devil who deceived them was thrown into the lake of fire
> and brimstone, where the beast and the false prophet are also; and
> they will be tormented day and night forever and ever (Rev. 20:10).

And finally on unredeemed humanity he added:

> And death and Hades were thrown into the lake of fire. This is the
> second death, the lake of fire. And if anyone's name was not found
> written in the book of life, he was thrown into the lake of fire (Rev.
> 20:14,15).

Jesus, when describing the last judgment, said of the final end
of the devil, his angels, and evil people:

> "Then He [the Son of Man] will also say to those on His left, 'Depart
> from Me, accursed ones, into the eternal fire which has been pre-
> pared for the devil and his angels' " (Matt. 25:41).

Can there be even the slightest shadow of doubt that the lake of
fire and brimstone about which John spoke is the same as the
eternal fire and Gehenna about which Jesus spoke? Assuredly
not.

Gehenna is hell, the final abode and punishment of the devil,
his hosts, and the unrighteous among men. That conclusion is
overwhelmingly clear.

Thus, the New Testament is frighteningly specific about hell.

14
The Infinity of Forever _____

A gang considers a robbery attempt of $5 million. All factors for success are fully evaluated. They conclude that the risk of getting caught is high. But $5 million is a lot of money. They wouldn't pull the job for $500,000, but for $5 million they'll risk it. They think ten to twenty years in prison is worth the gamble. Even if they're caught and must serve time, with the loot hidden away, they will live out their lives in luxury.

Similarly, those who reject the fact that hell is eternal are too often willing to risk living unrighteously in this life—wagering that the punishment to come will not be too great should they get "caught." Supported in such false ideas by many who disguise themselves as Christians, preachers, teachers, and theologians, many in our generation are gambling with odds that will devastate them and those who encouraged them in evil on the day of judgment.

How long does the punishment of the wicked endure? Forever? Can it be so severe that it is never ending? Two words, *forever* and *eternal,* answer those questions without doubt. Most emphatically, the punishment of the wicked is forever. This is clear in Scripture, and the orthodoxy of the church has always demanded an understanding of Scripture not one whit shy of that.

But because some, while acknowledging there is punishment for the ungodly, drone on for what seems like forever that *forever* does not mean forever, and that *eternal* does not not mean eternal, we must inquire into the meaning of the words *forever* and *eternal* as they are used in the Bible. Hell itself would burst into

157

singing if only the meaning of those words would change or if it could be shown that Christians for two thousand years have misunderstood them.

This issue of the duration of punishment for the unrighteous is *the* issue for professing Christians in the late twentieth century. Today there is hardly anyone feigning to be a Christian or assuming himself part of God's church who does not agree there is at least some judgment on the ungodly. But there is a growing number who are insisting that, contrary to the obvious teaching of the historic church, the Bible teaches only a temporary period of punishment.

Hiding under the guise of scholarship, too many theologians and biblical researchers have applied their newly invented linguistic hardware to "prove" that the words *forever* and *eternal* do not mean "endless." Emil Brunner, one of the more influential European theologians of this century and a party to this novel view, describes this method of interpretation as follows:

> Hence the expressions by which the New Testament emphasizes apparently the finality of the last judgment and of the damnation of the reprobate are so interpreted as to impart to judgment the character of a transitional stage, of a pedagogic cleansing process. Aionios [eternal] does not mean eternal, but only eschatological; the inextinguishable fire, the worm that dieth not, the apoleia, the destruction, the second death, etc.; all these unequivocal expressions are subjected to such a protracted process of exegetical chemistry that they lose the definiteness of their ultimate character.[1]

(This treatment of *aiōnios* is essentially the same as that used by Edward Fudge. See the discussion in Chapter 9.)

The idea of many moderns is that whatever punishment is meted out to the evil, it is temporary and amounts to nothing more than a learning process resulting ultimately in every one's becoming godly.

---

[1]*Eternal Hope* (Philadelphia: The Westminster Press, 1954), p. 183.

Such an idea as hell being temporary and remedial may be popular, but it surely doesn't fit the facts of the Bible. It is only the idle fancy of some who, for one reason or another, reject the teaching of Jesus Christ and His church. The meaning of the words *forever* and *eternal* cannot be bent that way.

Forever

The Greek used in the New Testament does not have a single adverb with the meaning the same as the English word *forever*. Instead, several similar phrases are used that incorporate the Greek word *aion* and that literally mean "into the ages." These phrases are translated into English as *forever* and *forever and ever*. These are the proper renderings of those phrases. It is so crucial to grasp how this expression is used that I will list the five places in Scripture where it is used concerning the punishment of the wicked:

> These men are those who are hidden reefs in your love-feasts when they feast with you without fear, caring for themselves; clouds without water, carried along by winds; autumn trees without fruit, doubly dead, uprooted; wild waves of the sea, casting up their own shame like foam; wandering stars, for whom the black darkness has been reserved forever (Jude 12,13).

> "And the smoke of their torment goes up forever and ever; and they have no rest day and night, those who worship the beast and his image, and whoever receives the mark of his name" (Rev. 14:11).

Of Babylon it is said:

> And a second time they said, "Hallelujah! Her smoke rises up forever and ever" (Rev. 19:3).

And of the devil it is said:

> And the devil who deceived them was thrown into the lake of fire and brimstone, where the beast and the false prophet are also; and they will be tormented day and night forever and ever (Rev. 20:10).

159

Though some translations leave off the word *forever* in 2 Peter 2:17, it is more than appropriate.

> These are wells without water, clouds that are carried with a tempest; to whom the mist of darkness is reserved for ever (KJV).

The Greek word *aion* is used some ninety-five times in the New Testament and with a variety of meanings. However, the plain, hard facts are that *whenever the word is used to designate a future period of time, it speaks of indefinite and unlimited time. Aion* is "an indefinite period of time; time without limitations, forever, time without end, eternity."[2]

Just four Scriptures will amply demonstrate that any attempt to limit this expression to a meaning of less than forever when it specifies a future period of time is completely in error.

> 1. For they exchanged the truth of God for a lie, and worshiped and served the creature rather than the Creator, who is blessed forever. Amen (Rom. 1:25).

Now who would be so foolish as to propose that God is only to be blessed for a limited period of time?

> 2. ". . . I was dead, and behold, I am alive forevermore . . ." (Rev. 1:18).

This is the resurrected Christ speaking. Surely it is unthinkable that He who is never to die again will be alive only until the end of a limited period of time!

> 3. "Put the word of the Lord abides forever" . . . (1 Pet. 1:25).

Imagine what that would mean if we understood forever to be anything but unending. God could then change His Word. That would make eternity a place of misery even for the righteous who would live in dread that He might alter His Word. That itself would be a form of eternal torment!

---

[2]Stuart, *Future Punishment,* p. 28.

4. "I am the living bread that came down out of heaven; if any one eats of this bread, he shall live forever . . ." (John 6:51).

If this "forever" spoken by Jesus is really a period of time with an end, then the blessedness of heaven for those in Christ is not forever. Again, that itself would be torment. That could not be. The reward of the righteous is eternal blessedness.

There is no way that "into the ages" in the Greek New Testament can mean anything but *forever* when that expression refers to the future. God is blessed forever, Jesus lives forever, God's Word abides forever, the people of God live forever, and the punishment of the wicked is forever.

Eternal

As we might anticipate, the Greek adjective, *aiōnios,* or "eternal," is also made a battleground by those who resist the everlastingness of God's judgment on the evil.

This common Greek word appears more than sixty-six times in the New Testament. In every single instance where it refers to a future time, *aiōnios* designates an endless period, a completely unlimited duration.

There are six Scripture portions where this word for eternal is used with respect to the retribution of the unrighteous. They are:

". . . it is better for you to enter life crippled or lame, than having two hands or feet, to be cast into the eternal fire" (Matt. 18:8).

". . .'Depart from Me, accursed ones, into the eternal fire which has been prepared for the devil and his angels' " (Matt. 25:41).

"And these go away into eternal punishment, but the righteous into eternal life" (Matt. 25:46).

"but whoever blasphemes against the Holy Spirit never has forgiveness, but is guilty of an eternal sin" (Mark 3:29).

And these will pay the penalty of eternal destruction, away from the presence of the Lord and from the glory of His power (2 Thess. 1:9).

> . . . let us proceed on to maturity, not laying again a foundation of repentance from dead works and of faith toward God, of instruction about washings, and laying on of hands, and the resurrection of the dead, and eternal judgment (Heb. 6:1,2).

The contention of those who oppose the forever punishment of the wicked here is that *eternal* doesn't mean "without end." They insist it means "eschatological," that is, it merely has general reference to the coming age. It refers to the "quality" of the age to come, but it has no reference to duration.

Such an argument is wishful thinking and is utterly lacking in responsible scholarship. But worse, it denies the truth of God. It has no basis in sound biblical scholarship nor in the interpretation of Scripture by the orthodox church. One can insist until he turns purple that the word *aiōnios* does not mean "eternal in duration," but that argument has no basis in fact. The attempt to foist such nonsense off on the people of God has about as much value as the plays a football team uses that work great in practice but don't work during a game when the real opposition is present and prepared. Biblical word games may be entertaining, but they do not change the meaning of words.

Consider just a few Scriptures where *aiōnios* speaks clearly of "unendingness," and where a mere reference to some quality of the age to come is a thoroughly inadequate interpretation.

> . . . according to the commandment of the eternal God . . . (Rom. 16:26).

Surely there is a quality of the age to come about God, but that is in no way what is in view here. It is the "unendingness" and everlastingness of God that Paul is speaking of.

> how much more will the blood of Christ, who through the eternal Spirit offered Himself without blemish to God . . . (Heb. 9:14).

Will the enemies of eternal punishment suggest that the Holy Spirit is not eternal but merely the eschatological Spirit? I'm sure some would! But the Spirit is eternal, and so will be the punishment of the wicked.

> . . . He became to all those who obey Him the source of eternal salvation (Heb. 5:9).

> ". . . that whoever believes in Him should not perish, but have eternal life" (John 3:16).

Will any who claim that the punishment of the wicked is limited dare suggest that salvation and everlasting life are also only a temporary transitional stage for the righteous? Transitional to what, pray tell? The same word that describes life as everlasting describes punishment as everlasting. What is true of the one must be true also of the other.

The evidence regarding the accuracy in rendering this word *aiōnios* as eternal is conclusive. Stuart summed it up thus:

> In regard to all the cases which have a relation to future time, it is quite plain and certain that they designate an endless period, an unlimited duration . . . if they have not the meaning which has just been stated, then the Scriptures do not decide that God is eternal, nor that the happiness of the righteous is without end, nor that His covenant of grace will always remain; a conclusion which would forever blast the hopes of Christians and shroud in more than midnight darkness all the glories of the gospel.[3]

Conclusion

The New Testament is totally unambiguous on the duration of "eternal" punishment. Not the slightest hint is to be found that the agony of hell will be one mite less than forever. Jesus, the One who is coming again to judge the living and the dead, expressed Himself clearly and without room for doubt about it. The rest of the New Testament writers followed His lead to the letter. Retribution for the ungodly is eternal, without end.

---

[3]Stuart, *Future Punishment*, p. 67.

Truly, those who have peddled the poison that neitherJesus nor the Scriptures teach such a doctrine have contributed greatly to the decline of hell. They have shaken the confidence of some with respect to the declarations of God. They have destroyed the wholesome fear of God in others. But the truth is unchanged. Any false hope of escaping the pains of an eternal hell other than through Jesus Christ is futile. God has spoken. He has plainly revealed the reality of eternal punishment, and along with it, the way it can be avoided by all who will accept God's way.

15
The Battle of the Kingdoms

The heart of the message preached in common by John the Baptist, the Lord Jesus Christ, the apostles of Christ, and the true church of God may be summed up in one sentence: "Repent, for the kingdom of God is at hand."

At least two things confront us in this statement—our need for repentance and our need for the kingdom of God, which is at hand. A denial or rejection of either of these needs will leave us in a very precarious and foolish position.

To "repent" means to say "Uncle." In other words, "I give; I surrender. I'm through running my life in my own way. I have been traveling a road that leads to hell and am now ready and willing to turn to the Lord and His kingdom." The kingdom of God relates to a realm or a government actively reigned over by the Lord Jesus Christ, and to turn to the Lord includes a turning to His government.

The kingdom of God, the government of God, the active reign of God, is expressed in two ways. First, it is to be experienced, lived in and under, in all its fulness in the age to come when Jesus Christ will reign with the Father and the Holy Spirit in divine splendor, glory, and grand perfection for all eternity. Secondly, the kingdom of God is not limited only to that future, eagerly awaited age to come. Right here and now, in this age, we are called by Christ to know and experience the first fruits of that kingdom. We are to taste the reign of Christ and experience His

165

lordship in this life. That present experience of the rule of Jesus Christ is found in the church. Established by Christ and actually built upon Him as the foundation, the church is not some nondescript, ethereal company of unrelated Christians. It is *the* concrete, definable, discernable, locatable place where He now reigns over His people on this earth as they await His physical return and the establishment of the kingdom in its fulness.

True repentance is an absolute prerequisite to coming under the active lordship of Christ. Unless one is under Christ's reign, he simply hasn't repented. He can be religious as the day is long and do all kinds of good things, but if he isn't experiencing Christ's rule, he has not repented as yet. Jesus Himself said, " 'You are My friends, if you do what I command you' " (John 15:14). And Paul sternly warned the Thessalonian Christians, "And if anyone does not obey our instruction in this letter, take special note of that man and do not associate with him, so that he may be put to shame" (2 Thess. 3:14).

It should be more than obvious then that repentance involves not only the reign of Christ in eternity, but also His reign in this age in the church. The letter to the Hebrews carries this powerful admonition: "Obey your leaders, and submit to them; for they keep watch over your souls, as those who will give an account. Let them do this with joy and not with grief, for this would be unprofitable for you" (Heb. 13:17). The experience of that reign, God's good government, begins in this life in the church. And when, so to speak, the dust settles in eternity, the question will be, "Who is in the kingdom of God?" Only those in that kingdom will be saved unto eternal life.

The Existence of Another Kingdom

This discussion of the kingdom of God suggests another topic. Since the kingdom of God exists with its subjects, is there another?

Yes, there is one other. It is the kingdom of darkness. This realm has its prince, Satan. Jesus called him the prince of this world. Two powerful forces reign in that realm with him: sin and death. All three, Satan, sin, and death, find expression in this present world. In speaking of the whole range of human history since the first man—Adam, Scripture declares concerning death: ". . . death reigned through the one [Adam] . . ." (Rom. 5:17). And with respect to sin, ". . . sin reigned in death . . ." (Rom. 5:21). And Jesus said of Satan, ". . . The ruler of this world is coming, and he has nothing in Me" (John 14:30). Yes, all three are presently reigning and ruling over the lives of their subjects.

What is the aim of their reign? To make you their subjects and to take you to hell with them! Hell is their certain doom for all eternity, but they will not be alone. Their subjects will be with them.

Perhaps you are thinking, "Do you mean to say that I will go to hell with them if I am a subject of their kingdom?" Most assuredly yes! Since their fate is sure, they are going to take as many to hell with them as possible. Listen to what the Scriptures declare about the final destination of the devil and death:

". . . the eternal fire which has been prepared for the devil and his angels" (Matt. 25:41).

And the devil who deceived them was thrown into the lake of fire and brimstone . . . and . . . will be tormented day and night forever and ever (Rev. 20:10).

"And death and Hades were thrown into the lake of fire . . ." (Rev. 20:14).

But these same passages also show that Satan and death will be joined in hell by their human subjects.

". . . Depart from Me, accursed ones [human beings], into the eternal fire which has been prepared for the devil and his angels" (Matt. 25:41).

167

> And the devil who deceived them [human beings] was thrown into the lake of fire and brimstone. . . . And I saw a great white throne and Him who sat upon it. . . . And I saw the dead, the great and the small, standing before the throne. . . . and they were judged, every one of them according to their deeds. And death and Hades were thrown into the lake of fire. . . . And if anyone's name was not found written in the book of life, he was thrown into the lake of fire (Rev. 20:10–15).

Deceit: Program of the King of Darkness

How will Satan and his agents, sin and death, manage to get so many people to follow them to hell? Primarily and fundamentally it will occur by deception. Arrogant and rebellious people, that is those who refuse to repent and obey the Lord God of heaven, are easily deceived. Many of these deceived people foolishly mock the existence of hell. But tragically they will laugh their way right into the place where their laughter will become weeping and gnashing of teeth.

Perhaps very few would end up in hell were it not for deception. Who would deliberately go to hell if he truly realized the terrors awaiting him? Even in the face of continual warnings from the Scriptures and the church, many people deliberately mock and deride hell's existence and act as though they are certain they could never wind up there—even if there were one. But on the day of their consignment to eternal punishment, no one will be able to deliver them despite their terrified screams.

Yes, Satan, with sin and death, continues to spin the web of deceit for rebellious and unrepentant people. Read carefully the following Scriptures concerning this drama of deception.

> And even if our gospel is veiled, it is veiled to those who are perishing, in whose case the god of this world has blinded the minds of the unbelieving, that they might not see the light of the gospel of the glory of Christ, who is the image of God (2 Cor. 4:3,4).

> But I am afraid, lest as the serpent *deceived* Eve by his craftiness, your minds should be led astray from the simplicity and purity of devotion to Christ (2 Cor. 11:3, italics mine).

And the great dragon was thrown down, the serpent of old who is called the devil and Satan, who *deceives* the whole world . . . (Rev. 12:9, italics mine).

And the devil who *deceived* them was thrown into the lake of fire . . ." (Rev. 20:10, italics mine).

But encourage one another day after day, as long as it is still called "Today," lest any of you be hardened by the *deceitfulness* of sin (Heb. 3:13, italics mine).

These Scriptures warn people of the deceit that is being practised on them, and unless they respond humbly, repent, and turn to God in faith, the day of judgment will overtake them and no deliverance will then be possible. As Isaiah the prophet said long ago concerning such, ". . . a *deceived* heart has turned him aside. And he cannot deliver himself . . ." (Isa. 44:20, italics mine). And again, "But because of your stubbornness and unrepentant heart you are storing up wrath for yourself in the day of wrath and revelation of the righteous judgment of God" (Rom. 2:5).

We need to understand this well. This drama of deceit is being staged by human actors and actresses. For the devil, sin, and death work through the willing instrumentation of men and women who themselves are deceived. As the Scriptures say, "But evil men and impostors will proceed from bad to worse, deceiving and being deceived" (2 Tim. 3:13). In fact, the deceived have believed a lie for so long that they would swear on a stack of Bibles that what they believe is true. They become self-righteously indignant any time their sincerity is challenged. Nevertheless, the kingdom of darkness operates through these dupes of the devil.

The Lord sternly warned about feigned righteousness and ceaseless contrivings to make people sons of hell, for that is in reality what the deceptive ones are doing. Jesus said: ". . . 'For you are like whitewashed tombs which on the outside appear beautiful, but inside they are full of dead men's bones and all uncleanness. Even so you too outwardly appear righteous to men, but inwardly you are full of hypocrisy and lawlessness' '' (Matt. 23:27,28). Again, ''. . . 'you travel about on sea and land to make one proselyte; and when he becomes one, you make him twice as much a son of hell as yourselves' '' (Matt. 23:15).

Some people are naively surprised to discover that such men and women actually operate in this world. In fact they disguise themselves so well that the undiscerning cannot detect the masquerade. But you can be sure that their doom is certain. The apostle Paul said of them: ''For such men are false apostles, deceitful workers, disguising themselves as apostles of Christ. And no wonder, for even Satan disguises himself as an angel of light. Therefore it is not surprising if his servants also disguise themselves as servants of righteousness; whose end shall be according to their deeds'' (2 Cor. 11:13–15).

Is it possible that these deceitful workers may be found occupying pulpits, conducting Bible studies and prayer sessions, pastoring churches, teaching in theological seminaries, speaking on radio and television, heading Christian organizations, leading denominations, and a whole host of other things? Undoubtedly, such positions and functions are high on Satan's placement priority list. And his people can come across as being such ''nice guys.'' Yet on the inside they are full of venom, rebellion, and deceit.

Warning against false facades, Jesus exhorted his disciples: '' 'Beware of the false prophets, who come to you in sheep's clothing, but inwardly are ravenous wolves' '' (Matt. 7:15). The deceived have the hardest time realizing that some so-called ministers and apparent Christian leaders could have these characteristics. ''Why he always seems to be so sweet and nice and unruffled about everything,'' some would say of a wolf dressed in white wool. Many an outwardly appearing ''nice guy'' is inwardly a ravenous wolf. That was Jesus' appraisal.

Therefore, as the kingdom of darkness carries on its program of deceit, many are being ensnared and led to impending judgment and doom. That entire kingdom will suffer eternal punishment in an appropriate place, a spot of thick darkness and blackness that defies the imagination. The apostle Peter called it the "pits of darkness" and "the black darkness" (2 Pet. 2:4,17). Yes, the kingdom of darkness is destined for darkness. Another word for the destination is hell.

You might say, "This sounds frightening." I hope it does, because a wholesome fear of hell is a good first step toward God. Those who have no such fear are pitiful members of the kingdom of darkness, and they all will end up in hell.

Transferring from Darkness to Light

Which kingdom are you in? This is the most important question of your life. If you are in the devil's kingdom, you need to admit that fact and undergo a change of kingdoms, a transfer to the kingdom of God. Human beings will spend eternity in one kingdom or the other, and that citizenship is established while we are in this life. If you should go to hell, it will be because you were in the kingdom of darkness in this life. That kingdom has no hope but hell. Are you presently one of its subjects? It's not too late to change. There is still time for deliverance. You may still be transferred from darkness to light, from deceit to truth.

You need to know that God ". . . is patient towards you, not wishing for any to perish but for all to come to repentance" (2 Pet. 3:9). You need not remain a subject of the kingdom of darkness. Only stubbornness and a refusal to repent can keep anyone there.

It is not unlikely that the most famous verse in the Bible is, "For God so loved the world, that He gave His only begotten Son, that whosoever believeth in Him should not perish, but have everlasting life" (John 3:16, KJV). There you have it, "should not perish . . ."—the very desire of the heart of God. God the Father sent His Son so that those who believe in Him might not perish. God provided a way out of hell. The eternal Father in heaven sent

His eternal Son as God incarnate—God in the flesh. God became a man.

The *Incarnation* means that the Son of God became a man in order to rescue us from the kingdom of darkness and bring us safely into the kingdom of God. The eternal Son of the Father thought enough of us that He condescended to assume human flesh on our behalf, and God the Father cared enough about our condition that He sent His Son into this world.

Jesus Christ did not have any personal need to become a man. After all, He is and always has been, before all ages, the only-begotten Son of the Father. All the glory and honor and power of the Father were and are His. Lacking nothing, He possessed all things. He is God of God, the Father's exact image, in all things the equal of His Father. Yet in love and pity for us, seeing our miserable condition and hell-bound direction—without ceasing to be God for even a moment—He genuinely became a man.

He entered this sin-stricken, guilt-ridden world to partake of its sin and guilt Himself in order to save those who would repent and turn to God. As the apostle Paul told us, "For you know the grace of our Lord Jesus Christ, that though He was rich, yet for your sake He became poor, that you through His poverty might become rich" (2 Cor. 8:9).

That's what Christmas is really all about. The eternal Son of God, who in His deity had no beginning of existence, was born of the Virgin Mary as a genuine human being. The Baby in the manger scene was none other than God incarnate, Immanuel—God with us. When the wise men found Mary, Joseph, and the Child in Bethlehem of Judea, they worshipped *the Child*. As the account says, "And they came into the house and saw the Child with Mary His mother; and they fell down and worshiped Him . . ." (Matt. 2:11). To worship anything or anyone other than the true God is idolatry. Yet, with God's approval, the wise men worshipped a Man, and it wasn't idolatry. Why? Because that Man was God of God, the second Person of the Trinity, who had become flesh for us.

Easter and the events preceding it also are centered in the Incarnation. Jesus the Child grew to manhood and at the age of thirty entered His public ministry after having been baptized by John the Baptist. For the next three years He went about doing good and preaching the gospel of the kingdom of God. He healed the sick, cast out demons, raised the dead, and performed many other miracles—so many in fact that the apostle John had to say: "And there are also many other things which Jesus did, which if they were written in detail, I suppose that even the world itself would not contain the books which were written" (John 21:25).

At the end of those three years He was betrayed by Judas Iscariot and underwent the mockery of several false trials before He was falsely condemned and crucified as a common criminal. But in His death He became an offering for sin on the behalf of all. "He was crucified, dead and buried," as the Apostles' Creed says.

Three days later He was raised again from the grave where He had been buried. Then, after having spent forty days with His apostles demonstrating the reality and truth of His Resurrection and explaining matters relating to the kingdom of God, He ascended to the Father to be crowned King of heaven. Together with the Father and the Holy Spirit, He is now actively reigning as King over His kingdom.

The Son of God did all these things in order to deliver us from the kingdom of darkness. Paul wrote joyously of the Father: "For He delivered us from the domain of darkness, and transferred us to the kingdom of His beloved Son" (Col. 1:13). In no other way can you or anyone be transferred from one kingdom to the other. He is the only way out, the only One who can save you from hell and make you a member of the kingdom of God.

Union with the King and the Kingdom

How is this transfer of kingdoms accomplished? It comes by faith through union with the King—Jesus Christ. Jesus said it was being born again—born from above (John 3:3). The eternal Son became a Man in order to join us to Himself and, through Himself

173

as mediator, to God. The whole human race had fallen into sin, death, and corruption. None was excepted. Human nature was sick and disease-ridden.

Jesus Christ assumed our human nature that He might join us to Himself and in that union bring about our cure. As He once said, ". . .'It is not those who are healthy who need a physician, but those who are sick; I did not come to call the righteous, but sinners' " (Mark 2:17). This curing of our sick nature takes place in union with Christ in His now glorified humanity.

The first step to bring about union with Christ to be taken is that of repentance and faith. ". . .'repent and believe in the gospel,' " said Jesus (Mark 1:15). We must recognize that we are in the wrong kingdom, living under the wrong rulers, namely, sin, death, and the devil.[1] We must realize that this kingdom, all of us included, is headed for eternal woe. Therefore, with genuine sorrow and humility we must turn to the true King, the Lord Jesus Christ, and believe in Him. We must believe in Him as the true Son of God sent by the Father to save us from sin, death, corruption, and the fire of hell.

The second step for us is to be baptized. Baptism is a sacrament which is administered by the one, holy, catholic, and apostolic church because baptism is under the authority of the church. " 'Go therefore and make disciples of all the nations, baptizing them in the name of the Father and the Son and the Holy Spirit' " (Matt. 28:19). The Lord gave the apostles His instructions to baptize, and at the same time gave them the authority to do so. They then carried on the establishment of His church and did as they were told. Those activities are forever the responsibility of His apostles and the churches descended from their labors. We are baptized in the name of the Father, the Son, and the Holy Spirit.

---

[1] For a full discussion of the two kingdoms, be sure to see my earlier book *It Ain't Gonna Reign No More* (Nashville: Thomas Nelson, 1978).

A third vital step in the cure of our souls through union with Christ is regular participation in the Eucharist, the Lord's Supper, Communion. In the Eucharist, the church worships the Lord with thanksgiving and partakes of the body and blood of Jesus Christ. A second-century bishop, Ignatius of Antioch, once called the Eucharist "the medicine of immortality." Our regenerated human nature is nourished through regular participation in the body and blood of the Lord. Indeed Jesus said, ". . . 'Truly, truly, I say to you, unless you eat the flesh of the Son of Man and drink His blood, you have no life in yourselves' " (John 6:53). That blessed table is vital to spiritual growth, and without it there is no spiritual life and power.

Many things could be said of union with Christ and of the benefits we receive. One of these is the line drawn between the kingdom of God and the kingdom of Darkness. " 'He who has believed and has been baptized shall be saved; but he who has disbelieved shall be condemned' " (Mark 16:16). Once you were in the kingdom of darkness, but now the Holy Spirit has brought you across that line into the kingdom of God. Baptism is a sure seal of that fact. No longer will you need doubt or wonder which kingdom you belong to.

Another benefit of this transfer between kingdoms is the assurance of the forgiveness of sins. The guilt that used to plague you is washed away, and the happy estate of sins forgiven is your portion. No one could adequately describe the blessed assurance of forgiveness, but King David came as close as the human tongue can when he joyously exclaimed: "How blessed is he whose transgression is forgiven, whose sin is covered! How blessed is the man to whom the Lord does not impute iniquity, And in whose spirit there is no deceit!" (Ps. 32:1,2).

A third benefit that is ours when we join faith to baptism is that union with Christ joins us with His resurrected, glorified human nature. In the words of Andrew Murray, ". . . in Romans 6 baptism is represented as the secret of the whole of sanctification, the entrance into a life in union with Jesus.''[2] We are united with Christ in His death and thus die to sin's reign over us. We are also united with Him in His burial and descend to hell with Him. In union with Him we are indeed delivered from the pains of hell. His Resurrection is also our portion as we are brought out from the grave to newness of life in victory over king death.

A fourth benefit of union with Christ is the gift of the Holy Spirit. Not only do the Father and the Son live in the church and its people, but the Holy Spirit does as well. On the very first day of the church, the day of Pentecost, Peter the apostle told the people gathered there: ''. . .'Repent, and let each of you be baptized in the name of Jesus Christ for the forgiveness of your sins; and you shall receive the gift of the Holy Spirit' '' (Acts 2:38). All three Persons indwell the church. Where the Father is, there is the Son, and where Father and Son are, there is the Holy Spirit. And as members of the body of Christ, we have the privilege of being ruled by the blessed Trinity.

No Excuses for Going to Hell

Can anything be so marvelous for man as God's provision for him to be delivered from the doom of eternal torment? How truly splendid and grand is God in His ways. If only we humans would spend our lives believing in and partaking of God's so-great salvation in Christ, how blessed we would be. *Instead of inventing complaints of how cruel and unjust hell is, we should come to faith and glory in how creative and gracious God's provision of deliverance from hell is!*

In the face of the brilliant light of salvation, it is no wonder that only the arrogant and unrepentant workers of iniquity will suffer the torments of hell. Consciously rejecting God and choosing to

---

[2]*The New Life,* revised edition (Minneapolis: Bethany Fellowship, 1965), p. 201.

go their own way, they plunge headlong towards doom. What needless folly! What a great waste! For there is no need for anyone to go to hell. God has given, to all who will receive it, a way of sure escape.

16
In My Flesh
I Will
See God _____

For I know that my Redeemer liveth,
and that he shall stand at the latter day
upon the earth.
And though after my skin
worms destroy this body,
Yet in my flesh shall I see God.
(Job 19:25,26; KJV).

Thus did that ancient patriarch Job express his confidence. How much did he know of the future and of the grand and glorious future of the people of God? We do not know. But we do know that he had the blessed hope. What he confessed is indeed also the hope of the church. The ultimate joy and blessedness for humanity is *to see God*.

Just as many torments await the reprobate, many glories await the redeemed. I look forward with trembling anticipation to them all. But I confess that above all else I want to see God, to behold Him in all His beauty and holiness. To that hope, above all else, we shall return again and again.

No book about hell could possibly be complete without speaking of the expectations of those whom God has justified—those who have been brought into union with Christ and who will thus make it past the judgment of God.

What is the reward for the righteous? Is it really worth it? These are questions with exciting answers. Though they can only be dealt with in part, even that part makes the hearts of God's people rejoice with joy unspeakable and full of glory.

The Resurrection of the Body

Of all the themes on which the apostle Paul wrote, he is most eloquent on that of the Resurrection. Here is but a sample:

> But if the Spirit of him who raised Jesus from the dead dwells in you, He who raised Christ Jesus from the dead will also give life to your mortal bodies through His Spirit who indwells you (Rom. 8:11).

And again:

> Behold, I tell you a mystery; we shall not all sleep, but we shall all be changed, in a moment, in the twinkling of an eye, at the last trumpet; for the trumpet will sound, and the dead will be raised imperishable, and we shall be changed. For this perishable must put on the imperishable, and this mortal must put on immortality. . . . then will come about the saying that is written, "Death is swallowed up in victory. O death, where is your victory? O death, where is your sting?" The sting of death is sin, and the power of sin is the law; but thanks be to God, who gives us the victory through our Lord Jesus Christ (1 Cor. 15:51–57).

Our human nature includes both body and soul. It would be a glorious thing if only the soul should be taken to be with God. But that is not the extent of His purpose. It is His will to redeem our whole being; that is even *more* glorious. Thus, Christ in His Incarnation fully took on human nature. When He was resurrected, His full humanity was there with a resurrected body to be felt and seen. Body and soul belong together. Because Christ is the glorious *first fruit,* we shout confidently with Job, "Yet in my flesh shall I see God!"

How much dare we to hope? Some might fear that, because the apostle Paul once spoke of "a spiritual body," we will inherit something intangible, an ethereal or unreal body. Yet to prevent such a fear, we have the very words of the Savior: ". . . 'Reach here your finger, and see My hands; and reach here your hand, and put it into My side; and be not unbelieving, but believing' '' (John 20:27).

Indeed Paul's phrase ''spiritual body'' refers to something else. Because Paul wanted us to be free from the fear that forever we would have to fight the battle of subduing fleshly lusts, he spoke of our resurrected body. He contrasted ''spiritual'' with ''natural'' so that we could know that the soul restored to God will possess a resurrected body completely attuned to the will of God.

Do you realize what that means? The lust of the flesh, concupiscence, that compulsive power to sin so familiar to us all, will be gone forever! We will be free at last! No longer will sin rise up bearing the disguise of legitimate bodily desires. Think of the relief that freedom from battle will bring. Augustine, who experienced first hand the white heat of the battle against passion, wrote: ''Just imagine how perfectly at peace and how strong will be the human spirit when there will be no passion to play the tyrant or the conqueror, no temptation even to test the spirit's strength.''[1]

Our resurrected body will be real! It will still be a human nature, but a glorified human nature, exactly what God intended for human nature from the very beginning. A wonderful transformation will have taken place, for these new bodies of ours will be incorruptible—no longer subject to sin, to illness, to injury, or to decay. We will possess that marvel of marvels, the age-old dream and hope of mankind: immortality.

Ponce de Leon was wrong. There is no fountain of youth. Who in his right mind would want to be young forever instead of being fully mature. For those made righteous by Christ, there is something far more grand than some illusive fountain of youth. They

---

[1]Augustine, *The City of God,* trans. Marcus Dods (New York: The Modern Library, 1950), 22.24.

have the promise of drinking from the eternal spring of the water of life without cost (Rev. 21:6).

We who have limped through life in bodies suffering from irreparable physical deterioration will experience a full vigor we have never known! Those who have gone through mortal life crippled, lame, blind, and infirm will possess perfected flesh. Men and women who endured torture and felt the pain and loss of crippling destruction will be restored to a condition better than they ever knew.

What reassurance to know that we have been ". . . born again to a living hope through the resurrection of Jesus Christ from the dead, to obtain an inheritance which is imperishable and undefiled and will not fade away . . ." (1 Pet. 1:3,4). Even in this alone there is hope enough to strengthen us in our pilgrimage through the trials of life. But this is just the beginning.

Joys of the Redeemed

Through the senses of our new and marvelous bodies we will experience beauty beyond anything ever imagined by mankind. The apostle John described a glorious city, the New Jerusalem, for the redeemed (Rev. 21). And there will be a new song (Rev. 14:3) that only the people of God can sing!

Nor will ours be a lonely joy. Our resurrection will be no more individualistic than our pilgrimage on earth. The church, the body of Christ, the holy temple, the bride of Christ will rejoice in her union together with Christ. Our rejoicing *together* will blend in harmony of song far richer than the sum of mere individual voices. We will find ourselves experiencing the fulfillment of the fact that each of us is eternally a truly functioning member of the body that shares the glorious humanity of its Head. We will all be living stones, the very dwelling of God in the Spirit. Eternally, we will each have our part in the bride that receives the love, nurture, and care of the Bridegroom.

181

Friendships begun here will grow and blossom there. Fellowship with our brothers and sisters will be unbroken and beyond comparison. Transparency will be complete and we will know and be known—absolutely. Such a union of perfect love will exist as humanity has never seen. In the eternal home of the children of God, His completed family will gather in communion such as no earthly love song could dare to describe. There we will meet the ancients who we now know by their works, but then we will know them by sight. Then through endless ages we will join together in the service of God, resting, yes, but not idle. For His kingdom is forever.

Strangely, popular culture tends to picture heaven as a place of idleness. We've all seen the cartoons of people with wings sitting on clouds and strumming harps. But such is far from the case. Instead, the whole creation, groaning throughout the ages as it awaited the revealing of the sons of God (Rom. 8:19–21), will then experience redemption. The perfect purpose and fulfillment of every created thing will be realized forever. There will be no boredom, no frustration, no inability to achieve. In eternity we will see for the first time what God intended for each part of His manifold creation.

The New Jerusalem

There will be no more glorious landmark in heaven than the city of New Jerusalem, the community of the redeemed. For there the church will have come to fruition as the city ". . . whose architect and builder is God" (Heb. 11:10) and will be revealed as the bride of the Lamb.

The children of God will receive their long-awaited inheritance. Their city, the King's city, will shine in a glory and brilliance that demonstrates the bond of their attachment to Him. John, seeking to describe it, could only speak in terms of gold, silver, and gems, for this is the ultimate inheritance—that of the children of the King.

182

Ugly and terrible things will not be found in New Jerusalem. Death is banished along with the fear of it. Mourning, crying, and pain will be gone. We will have suffered our last loss. Of our sins we will remember only that we are rid of them. Of the everlasting punishment of the wicked we will feel only happiness that we are not among them.

Immorality, lying, and all evil will no longer pose any kind of threat. No longer will the people of God be embarrassed or polluted by its presence. They will no longer even have to watch the wicked practice their abominations. Nothing like that will ever come into the Holy City.

The Lamb, the Bridegroom, our Lord Jesus Christ, will be there, united with His bride, His prayer of long ago now fulfilled: " 'Father, I desire that they also, whom Thou hast given Me, be with Me where I am, in order that they may behold My glory, which Thou hast given Me; for Thou didst love Me before the foundation of the world' " (John 17:24). All His faithful people who through the long ages have desired to be with Him will be gathered to His bosom. And indeed they will behold His glory! He has promised many mansions, and here in the midst of purity, peace, joy, and light, that promise will be kept.

Face to Face We Shall Behold Him

I said that the ultimate, the pinnacle of eternity will be to actually *see God*. As we shall note, this is not just a private opinion. The truth is that the major desire of each and every human being should be to see God and be with Him forever. That vision is to be everyone's pearl of great price. Nevertheless, people get dragged away by the allurements of this world that appear so lustrous for a time, and for many people the blessed hope becomes only a vague and transitory wish.

In His message called the Sermon on the Mount, Jesus Christ laid a simple promise before His disciples:

"Blessed are the pure in heart, for they shall see God" (Matt. 5:8).

183

For those who are earnest, the prospect of seeing God is a great motivator for holiness. Once truly grasped by the children of God, cleansing will result. As the apostle John said,

> Beloved, now we are the children of God, and it has not appeared as yet what we shall be. We know that, when He appears, we shall be like Him, because we shall see Him just as He is. And every one who has this hope fixed on Him purifies himself, just as He is pure (1 John 3:2,3).

Between human beings and this great vision of God stands a division point: the Judgment Day. And Jesus Christ is the Judge. We must get past God's throne of judgment to see God.

The Great Day of Judgment

In the great day of judgment, Jesus Christ will issue a call and all the dead will be resurrected (see John 5:25–29). That's right! There's a time coming when a command will be addressed to all the dead. Some will be resurrected to life and some to judgment. Those who are redeemed will be judged, but they will enter eternal life. As we have already clearly shown, the wicked will be judged and enter eternal condemnation.

It is the Son of Man who calls and judges. Why can He do these things? Because He has the very same life as the Father, a life that carries authority over death. Remember that this coequal and undivided life has belonged to the Son from before all ages. He has the same authority as the Father, an authority that death cannot disobey. So the dead will obediently come forward for judgment.

At that day (would that it were today!), a most awesome sight will greet both the living and the dead:

> "But when the Son of Man comes in His glory, and all the angels with Him, then He will sit on His glorious throne. And all the nations will be gathered before Him; and He will separate them from one another, as the shepherd separates the sheep from the goats; and He will put the sheep on His right, and the goats on the left. Then the

184

King will say to those on His right, 'Come, you who are blessed of
My Father, inherit the kingdom prepared for you from the foundation of the world. . . .'

"Then He will say to those on His left, 'Depart from Me, accursed
ones, into the eternal fire which has been prepared for the devil and
his angels. . . .'

"And these will go away into eternal punishment, but the righteous into eternal life" (Matt. 25:31–34,41,46).

As we have shown, that resurrection from the dead will be a
bodily resurrection. All human beings will exist forever, but not
as bodiless spirits. At *this* resurrection all departed spirits will be
reunited with their resurrected bodies.

So, when all the hosts of humanity are finally gathered before
the Judge, they will stand there in real human flesh. And with real
human eyes they will look up and gaze at the Son of Man. When
they see Him, those who are the "sheep" will be excited with joy,
and they will inherit the kingdom prepared for them. But those
who are the "goats" will be filled with hysterical terror, because
they are the ones who will be sent off into eternal punishment.

It is the heart that Christ will judge on that great day. When
someone does something that looks good outwardly, but is done
for the wrong reason, it is sin. Many people do their good deeds
for their own personal pleasure or because of greed or
ambition—not for God. Well, Christ will judge whether something that looks virtuous actually serves good or evil.

But there is also a second aspect of anyone's works that God
will take into account in deciding whether they are truly good.
There is a difference between doing something to attempt to
appease God, and doing something out of a pure heart led by His
Spirit. As the apostle Paul put it, ". . . love from a pure heart and
a good conscience and a sincere faith" (1 Tim. 1:5). ". . . without
faith it is impossible to please Him" (Heb. 11:6). I think the point
is made. Those who sincerely want to see God learn from Him
how to behave. Those who are against Him decide on their own.

One more comment from Augustine:

> The Catholic faith distinguishes the just from the unjust not by the law of works but by the law of faith, without which works which seem good are turned into sins.[2]

The Judge in the Form of Man

The unrighteous, those to whom we have given so much attention in this book, will see Jesus Christ only in the form of a Man, not in that form by which He is equal to the Father. We need to remember:

> "Blessed are the pure in heart, for they shall see God" (Matt. 5:8).

That statement has an obvious corollary: "Miserable are the impure in heart, for they shall *not* see God."

The vision itself is face to face (1 Cor. 13:12) and promised to the righteous as their ultimate reward:

> . . . I will love him, and will manifest myself to him (John 14:21, KJV).

Obviously, that vision is so precious that the wicked will not have it. Characteristic of the whole of their lives, their eyes are to be blinded so that they will not see God even in the incarnate Son. If they were able to see Him as God, there would be nothing special about His promise that those who are pure in heart would be so blessed to see Him.

No one will see the Father in that last and final judgment. But all will see the Son, because He is also Man. Even the wicked will see Him. Yes, the Father will judge through the Son—the One to whom He handed judgment. And though that Son will appear there as Man rather than God, His appearance will be no less terrifying to the wicked, and no less welcome to the pure of heart, for He promised:

---

[2]Augustine *Against Two Letters of the Pelegians* III. 5.

"Truly, truly, I say to you, he who hears My word, and believes Him who sent Me, has eternal life, and does not come into judgment, but has passed out of death into life" (John 5:24).

Still, that vision of Him as Son of Man that He prophesied for those who believe will be only the beginning of blessings for the righteous. For next they will hear Him say to them, ". . .'Come, you who are blessed of My Father, inherit the kingdom prepared for you from the foundation of the world' " (Matt. 25:34). So as the wicked set out weeping, wailing, gnashing their teeth, and headed for everlasting torment, the righteous will begin the glorious eternity of everlasting life.

Knowing Father, Son, and Holy Spirit

We can know God in this life, as believers throughout the ages have testified, but we do not have that direct face-to-face vision. Gregory the Great said it well:

Whatever progress anyone may have made while placed in this life, he cannot yet see God by vision, but obscurely and in a mirror. . . . But if He were already perfectly seen, surely He would not be seen, as it were, in darkness. But because He is neither entirely seen, nor again, entirely not seen, it is rightly said that God is seen from afar.[3]

So, passing from the judgment, the righteous will experience the fulfillment of the Psalm:

Thou wilt make known to me the path of life;
In thy presence is fulness of joy;
In Thy right hand there are pleasures forever (Ps. 16:11).

That joy will be the most complete ever known, nothing can conceivably be added to it, because there is nothing more to want. Augustine put the point quite clearly when he wrote:

---

[3]*Moralia Praefatio* 31.51.101, quoted in Joseph P. McClain, *The Doctrine of Heaven in the Writings of Saint Gregory the Great* (Washington, D.C.: Catholic University of America Press, 1956), p. 27.

Philip had grasped this correctly so that he said to the Lord: "Show us the Father, and it is enough for us." (John 14:8). But he did not yet realize that he could have also said the very same thing in this way: "Lord show us yourself and it is enough for us." . . . Therefore, whether we hear: "Show us the Son," or "Show us the Father," the one has just as much force as the other. For they are one, as He Himself declares: "I and the Father are one." (John 10:30). Finally, on account of their very inseparability it suffices at times to name the Father alone, or the Son alone, as the one whose countenance will fill us with joy.[4]

But the righteous will behold not just Father and Son, but the Holy Spirit as well. It is God the three in one in whose image we have been made. We will see all three Persons in their united glory. Gregory the Great expressed well that heavenly vision:

Then we shall clearly see how three, although divisible are one; and how one, although indivisible, is three. The tongue of God, therefore, who then speaks, is the visible clarity of God exalting us.[5]

Thus, the human creature at long last will experience in ultimate relationship with God the final fulfillment of the promise that His people should ". . . become partakers of the divine nature. . ." (2 Pet. 1:4). That eternal partaking will be the source of such joy that the elect will not be able to contain it. Gregory again is a good source of a description of that joy, as he commented on Job 8:21 (" 'He will yet fill your mouth with laughter, and your lips with shouting.' "):

When all the elect are filled by the joy of the clear contemplation of the beatific vision, they, as it were, break forth into laughter in the mouth of the mind. We call it a shout of joy when we conceive such joy in the heart that we are incapable of expressing it in words. The voice, however, expresses this exultation of the mind which cannot be set forth in words. The mouth is rightly said to be filled with laughter and the lips with rejoicing, because in the eternal fatherland, when the mind of the just is carried away in exultation, the

---

[4]Augustine *On the Trinity* I.8(17).
[5]*Moralia Praefatio* 30.4.17, quoted in McClain, *Doctrine of Heaven*, p. 36.

voice is lifted up in a song of praise. They, who see so much that they are incapable of expressing it, shout with laughter because, without encompassing it, they sing about what they love.[6]

One thing we can be sure of is that the joy of God's people will increase without limit forever and ever and ever, never to stop. For as our knowledge of God increases, it will lead us into greater and greater happiness and fulfillment. In that great city we will grow and grow in an intimate relationship with the King of kings as He reveals Himself to us.

To Him That Overcometh

Living in the midst of the hassles and problems of life, we easily lose sight of the beatific vision. We often forget that we want to see God. But let's never forget to persevere! The apostle John said over and over again that God has rewards for the "overcomer." The victor will,

" '. . . eat of the tree of life . . .' " (Rev. 2:7).

" '. . . not be hurt by the second death' " (Rev. 2:11).

". . . eat of the hidden manna . . . and [be given] a new name . . ." (Rev. 2:17, KJV).

" '. . . [be given] authority over the nations' " (Rev. 2:26).

" '. . . be clothed in white garments. . .' " (Rev. 3:5).

" '. . . [be made] a pillar in the temple of . . . God . . .' " (Rev. 3:12).

" '. . . sit [with Christ] on [His] throne . . .' " (Rev. 3:21).

Indeed, we find perseverance and faithfulness to be so very characteristic of the lives of those who look forward to being with the Lord. Speaking of the driving dynamic of his own life, Saint

---

[6]*Moralia Praefatio* 8. 52. 88, quoted in McClain, *Doctrine of Heaven*, p. 48.

Paul said: "I press on toward the goal for the prize of the upward call of God in Christ Jesus" (Phil. 3:14).

James, the brother of the Lord, exhorted the Christians experiencing trial to endure for, "Blessed is a man who perseveres under trial; for once he has been approved, he will receive the crown of life, which the Lord has promised to those who love Him" (James 1:12).

And finally, among the very last words we have from Jesus are these: " 'Behold, I am coming quickly, and my reward is with Me, to render to every man according to what he has done' " (Rev. 22:12).

Let us then, brothers and sisters, keep on in faith and works, aiming for that resurrection of life. For we have a promise: We shall see God and we shall reign with Him. There is no comparable goal, and it is offered to the overcomers.

With Job, let us cling with confidence to the greatest hope mankind can ever know: "In my flesh I shall see God!"

Bibliography

Alger, W. R. *A Critical History of the Doctrine of a Future Life*. Boston: Roberts Bros., 1880.

Baird, J. Arthur. *The Justice of God in the Teaching of Jesus*. Philadelphia: Westminster Press, 1963.

Berdyaev, Nicolas. *The Destiny of Man*. London: Geoffery Bless, 1957.

Brunner, Emil. *Eternal Hope*. Philadelphia: The Westminster Press, 1954.

Buis, Harry. *The Doctrine of Eternal Punishment*. Philadelphia: Presbyterian and Reformed, 1957.

Bultmann, Rudolph. *Theology of the New Testament,* vol. 1. New York: Scribner, 1951–1955.

Darwin, Charles. *Autobiography of Charles Darwin*. London: Collins, 1958 edition.

Farrar, F. W. *Eternal Hope*. New York: E. P. Dutton & Company, 1878.

Farrar, F. W. *Mercy and Judgment*. New York: E. P. Dutton & Company, 1881.

Hick, John. *Death and Eternal Life*. London: Collins, 1976.

Horberry, Matthew. *Works, An Enquiry Into The Scripture Doctrine of Future Punishment*. Oxford: Clarendon Press, 1828.

Martin, James Perry. *The Last Judgment in Protestant Theology from Orthodoxy to Ritschl*. Grand Rapids: Eerdmans, 1963.

Maurice, F. D. *Theological Essays,* 3rd ed. London: Macmillan, 1871.

Mill, John Stuart. *Three Essays On Religion,* 3rd ed. London: Longmans, Green, 1885.

Motyer, J. O. *After Death A Sure and Certain Hope.* Philadelphia: Westminster Press, 1965.

Pieper, Franz August. *Christian Dogmatics,* vol. 3. St. Louis: Concordia Publishing House, 1953.

Pusey, Edward Bouverie. *What Is of Faith as to Everlasting Punishment?* 2nd ed. Oxford: J. Parker, 1880.

Remensnyder, Junius Benjamin. *Doom Eternal.* Chicago: Funk & Wagnalls, 1887.

Robinson, John A. T. *But This I Can't Believe.* New York: The New American Library, 1967.

Robinson, John A. T. *Jesus and His Coming.* New York: Abingdon Press, 1958.

Rowell, Geoffery. *Hell and the Victorians.* Oxford: Clarendon Press, 1974.

Shedd, William T. *The Doctrine of Endless Punishment.* New York: Charles Scribner's Sons, 1886.

Stuart, Moses. *Future Punishment.* Philadelphia: Presbyterian Publication Committee, 1867.

Walker, Daniel P. *The Decline of Hell.* London: Rontledge and Kegan Paul, 1964.

Weatherhead, Leslie. *The After World of the Poets.* London: Epworth Press, 1937.

Whittemore, T. *The Modern History of Universalism from the Era of the Reformation to the Present Time.* Boston: Author, 1830.

Index of Bible References

Index _____

Reward of the righteous, 178
Robinson, John A. T., 33, 36, 54, 146
Roman Catholic attitude, 20ff.

S

Salvation, 176
Satan, 168ff.
Schleirmacher, Friedrich, 126
Scholasticism, 69ff., 75
Scotus Erigena, 34, 119
Scripture,
    interpretation of on hell, 44ff.
Second Helvetic Confession, 113
Shedd, William T., 136
Sheol, 131ff.
Shepard, Thomas, 84ff.
"Sinners in the Hands of An Angry God," 80–82
Socinians, 32
Socinus, Faustus, 120
Strauss, D. F., 53
Stuart, Moses, 137n., 160, 163

T

Tarturus, 147, 151ff.
Tennyson, 50
Tertullian, 107
Tractarians, 128

U

Unitarianism, 124ff.
Universalism, 32, 40ff., 51, 54, 55ff.
    history of, 116ff.
    scriptural support for, 45ff.